Praise
Blessings for Your Students

"A beautiful meditation on the power of naming and the opportunity to reflect deeply, across all axes of differences, on college and university campuses today."
   —Wendy Cadge, dean of the Graduate School of Arts and Sciences and professor of humanistic social sciences at Brandeis University

"The gift of Dr. Jan Fuller's words to inspire other chaplains and those called on to provide blessings on campus will be a wonderful resource. *Blessings for Your Students* is a powerful teaching tool for all those who find themselves at the microphone with a desire to be inclusive and share the impactful presence of love in our work on college campuses."
   —Connie Book, president of Elon University

"Jan's prayers are truly exceptional. This book gives college and university leaders and chaplains an extraordinary resource. When you are trying to find the right words for important campus celebrations or devastating community losses, this is an invaluable resource, as well as inspiration for your own spiritual centering."
   —Nancy Oliver Gray, president emerita of Hollins University

"May the blessings in this marvelous volume be heard by all those who deserve them—which is all of us. The two prayers 'A Vision for a New Class' and 'For the Wonder of Music' alone are enough to have the volume open on your desk or nightstand and there are many, many more within."
   —Bill Gordh, director of expressive arts and chapel at The Episcopal School in the City of New York and author of *Building a Children's Chapel: One Story at a Time*

"Speaking sacred words in religiously diverse and secular spaces is one of the persistent challenges of contemporary higher education chaplaincy. Not only are Fuller's blessings inclusive and adaptable, they're also rhetorically elegant—a wonderful resource for the field!"

—**Adam Kirtley, interfaith chaplain of Whitman College**

Blessings for Your Students

Blessings for Your Students

PRAYERS FOR INTERFAITH COMMUNITIES IN HIGHER EDUCATION

JANET FULLER

Church Publishing Incorporated
19 East 34th Street
New York, NY 10016
www.churchpublishing.org

Cover design and typeset by Nord Compo

A record of this book is available from the Library of Congress.

ISBN 978-1-64065-667-3 (pbk)
ISBN 978-1-64065-668-0 (ebook)

Contents

A Blessing
for This Book

May those whose hands
and eyes and ears
touch these pages and words
find them full and shaped with heart,
feel them real, rough, and hewn by hope,
sense in them leaders who have sought the common good
and found wisdom, joy, and insight.

May those who breathe these words
be touched by the wordless spirit
whose graces are found in wind and silence,
in laughter and humanity.

Blessed be those
who receive these prayers.
Blessed be the communities
who hear them spoken,
whose beginnings and endings, celebrations and sorrows,
bind them up and send them forward.

Blessed be those who need a prayer, an inspiration, a drop
    of awe
to quiet,
to stir,
or name,
to bring us together

with mind and heart,
whole and just and able,
with you in our midst
in our moment
in a prayer
in empty open hands
in a word.

May it be.

Preface

The year I turned eleven I was called to be a higher education chaplain, although it was years before I could fathom or name this calling. I remember weeping bitterly on my bed, aware—even at that tender age—that I would be obliged to choose between being smart and being faithful. It was a subtle sense, one I cannot quite retrace. The silence of my Sunday school teachers in the face of my frequent questions. The inability of my pastors to respond to my queries. The sense that my presence in youth group challenged adults' plans because I wanted to understand more deeply. But I understood already that too many questions disturbed others, especially my elders, and that it was my obligation—especially as a girl—to trust and obey. I did not need to understand more, their responses communicated; my brain and intellect (however small and adequate) were not to be trusted, my emotions were not to direct me. To think for myself was rebellion. My well-educated and thoughtful parents were, of course, horrified at the message I had comprehended, as it did not at all exemplify their commitments and faith. And I began to understand that many other children and young adults felt similar anti-intellectual bents to their Christian experience. Some theology is difficult to explain, mysterious to encounter, and it may seem simpler to offer the platitude "just believe it" or "you'll understand later."

I was in college before I began to see and believe otherwise. In those years, I began to perceive, through a chaplain, that faith served the intellect and that thinking, asking and answering, and digging deeply into the whys and hows served faith. Thinking was useful and productive to spiritual growth. So were emotion and all the senses. In that blessed discovery there was enormous relief. It was no longer necessary to choose the rebel way; I could trust science and philosophy, God, and my whole self too.

Thus began a journey into higher education chaplaincy, which I trace back to too many hard questions of those who could offer few answers or directions. It became clear that others were like me—checking their faith at the gate of a university or at the door of a classroom, closing off their minds at the beginning of a religious meeting. I was drawn to those students, and I wanted to be among them, offering them the same blessed opportunity for reintegration and relief, with the invitation to include all of themselves in the journey of faith, thought, and wholeness. I wanted to be in the institutions where those discoveries could be made and supported.

The mystery is that we are loved as we are, whole and fragmented too, but that we are created to be whole and balanced.

It seems important to share here that—into my early 20s—I lived in the Middle East, a Christian minority among Muslims. My own spiritual language was shaped, beyond the heart and mind distinctions, by those in my family and neighborhood whose devotion did not look or sound like mine. My ears became sensitive to those who were excluded in some ways of speaking, or in the language itself. My own prayers of childhood were also modeled after petitions I learned across the street with my Muslim friends, in words that need translating, but that sound like poetry. And in divinity school I was touched by the sanctity of the Holy Name—and the adaptations of Jewish communities and teachers to experience as personal and present such a transcendent and powerful relationship by many names. My dear professor and mentor—Luke Timothy Johnson—reminded me one afternoon that I might want to shut up and be silent to give God a way to get a word in edgewise. Those silences carried me into the presence of the Holy, more than any words could do, and I now urge chaplains to utilize the power of silence in the process of writing and speaking blessings over our communities.

Early in my chaplaincy career of 40 years, I began to write my own prayers. My first degree was in literature and poetry, a love that has remained constant, and it was the perfect foundation for theology and scripture, and for the studies and arts of ministry. The extemporaneous prayers of my childhood would not hold up to the scrutiny of an academic community of whom many were philosophers and poets. The Book of Common Prayer and other church resources offered nothing for the communities of students and academics who were spiritually diverse. I needed prayers that weren't terribly religious in those traditional ways, words for expressing yearnings that engaged our hearts and minds, that brought us together and acknowledged a great variety of souls, bodies, and ways of being. I sought language that included women, arts, wonderings, even questions. I experimented with ways to speak truth for a community in phrasings that sounded more like poetry than prayer, though, honestly, these were equivalent for me. Prayers came to me in verse, for ease on the eye and breath, and because they come from the poetic spirit in me.

Delivering a prayer is more than reading words from a page. It asks of us to embody those words, to offer our hearts in the blessing, to hold our wholeness as evidence of the Presence toward whom we point and yearn.

In my first year at one university (where I was astonished to learn that the chaplain was to offer prayer/meditation before faculty meetings), I did my duty, without having quite yet found my voice for that community. At the second faculty meeting, the minutes of that first faculty meeting were read—with raucous laughter and the motion to correct them—"The chaplain delivered the medication." It became a phrase and idea I came back to often over the years. An opening meditation or prayer or blessing was not to placate or to appease, not to medicate us into submission or sleep, not to do anything to the faculty or participants. It was a moment to perceive our wholeness, our sacred mission as scholars, mentors, teachers, and learners. A blessing is a moment to be tender, to permit our hearts to be open and awake, to be where and as we are, to acknowledge our humanity, our snark, our joy, and to be one body even for one moment.

Sometimes it feels, on the one hand, as if prayer at a campus occasion is offered as a medication, something bitter to be swallowed for our own good, something to endure until we can get to the good stuff. On the other hand, I have accepted the opportunities to create and offer a small moment of reflection, perhaps a small gem, a sense of the heart and mind held together in some peace, in which a community acknowledges its unity, its existence, its dependence on each other and those we have not yet met, and others who are ethereal to us but as real as we are. Sometimes, it is an opportunity to simply look in the mirror and to remember that we, too, are loved.

Blessings are for the community, and yet they are perhaps addressed to something or someone larger than one university gathering or community or faculty. In a symbolic way, we place ourselves to call attention to ourselves in the eye of One or Another who is larger and more powerful, who has another way of being and seeing. If this is God, then we ask God to see us as we really are. If Spirit or Love or Life or Energy, we give ourselves over to Her for a moment, to receive the blessings available. We are seen each from our unique perspectives—the gathering of students presented to the Holy, and the Holy perceived by humans. The chaplain stands between them, speaking the mystery into awareness. It's not magic. It requires discipline of language, thought, and process. It asks playfulness and experimentation.

What I have compiled in this small volume is a series of blessings I have offered in public—in large and small gatherings—and in private with one person or a small group. They are the yearnings from my own heart and mind, words from my own abyss or joy, spoken over experiences and events and people that touched me deeply. While my heart and mind are much more at union than when I was 11 or 21, these blessings still invite us to hold together what is fragmented, what needs healing and understanding, all that is still tender and lovely.

I offer them in hopes that they will become useful in being community, naming pain and joy—sometimes in the same moment—honesty and spirit, without necessity for the kind of religious language that can be experienced as "conversation stoppers." Finally, I offer these blessings in hopes of articulating gratitude even before it occurs to us to feel thankful.

A Note on Interfaith Blessings

The blessings I have compiled in this volume are less interfaith than the contexts in which they were and will be offered. There are multiple ways to think of interfaith, one of which might be a series of contrasting and mirroring ideas, speaking to multiple frames of reference. These blessings have certainly been written for interfaith or gatherings and communities where many points of view enhance the hearing. The context of the blessings matters. I believe that they will be useful in many communities where the audience is diverse, plural, secular, or willing to hear new ideas.

How to Use This Book

Six chapters aim to organize blessings thematically, although I recognize that there is much overlap. Chaplains preside over transitions of every kind: from arrival on campus to departure at commencement, new programs and initiatives, hopes as they evolve, students as they change their identities and even their names (Chapter One). Much of what is in the first chapter could also be adapted and used for special occasions—opening convocations, commencements, farewell dinners, and welcoming events. In crisis, chaplains are worth their weight in gold, managing rituals and meaning-making moments for those who are struggling. The death of a member of the campus community is only one such moment where a chaplain must speak for and to the hearts of many (Chapter Two). As university communities seek to prioritize justice movements and initiatives, as we initiate and support the work of equity, we bless those who advocate for the good as we also invite self-reflection (Chapter Three). It falls to the chaplain sometimes to point out wonders or to name hopes as they become evident on the horizon, on behalf of a community. We bring to awareness beauty, wonder at our fingertips, at our feet, in our line of sight, or often coming to birth in our corporate or unique lives (Chapter Four). The spirituality of gratitude might be a book of its own, but we can and should speak to the joys and successes, as well as the optimism and gratefulness of the community in so many moments and ways, even in the midst of struggle (Chapter Five). The final chapter includes prayers for particular campus occasions and events that are common in higher education: convocations for honors, capital campaigns, dedication of buildings and programs, moments of ending and beginning, even trustees' meetings (Chapter Six).

I can imagine a chaplain, teacher, campus minister, administrator—and many others, to be honest—picking up this book and finding it a blessing in their own journey to be centered and whole. It will be helpful for those newly in public leadership who desire models of attempts to be inclusive of many worldviews. I can also imagine yearning souls, who love prayer blessings and are looking for new ways to experience the spirit, poring over a prayer here and there in these pages.

I have removed the identifying particularities where they might once have been, as an invitation to find words, phrases, and ideas that inspire your own writing, thinking, or praying process. You might insert the names of your own campuses or communities, even students or faculty. Some of us write more easily than others and need examples. I will offer suggestions, in the next section, as to adapting blessings for particular communities or needs. Sometimes a word will take flight, as many of my blessings did after a rainstorm, or a bird call, or a snowfall. Blessings for individuals have one initial, as an invitation to insert a name of your choosing.

Notes on Naming
and to Whom We Pray

A prayer at an event is rarely "filler," and it is put there for a reason, in the same way it would be offered in a private setting. It helps us bless the event or a person well when we understand or discern the purpose of prayer or blessing. Depending on the occasion, a recognizable prayer is necessary. Other times we speak to the collective, drawing us together, acknowledging our commonality, purpose, and direction. The person offering the prayer or blessing needs to ascertain the occasion, the need, the opportunity. This entails listening to the community and the heart, silent preparation, following your intuition, and finding words to name what is real.

There are as many ways to name the Divine, the source, the fountain of all being, as your heart or community allows. It will be important, for student populations who tend to be less religious but as spiritual as the rest of the population, to mix it up, to vary your openings. It's also perfectly suitable, sometimes, not to name any One or Thing, just to speak the moment into consciousness, to acknowledge the reality of the time you are in and addressing, to invite the collaboration of the energy of the universe and the community gathered. There might be an implied deity, or none, the universe or energy, the gathered and those of the ether. Of course, in traditional settings, it is proper to use the usual and acceptable attributions, but I have avoided them here, opting for sometimes unothodox naming for better inclusion and to stimulate our imaginations and spirits. On campuses where there are many who follow polytheistic traditions, and in particularly secular communities or moments, it will be inappropriate to name the divine at all or to assume that God is One. In that case, the "One" who is addressed often in these blessings will need to be shifted to a more universal spirit and we can be substituted for you. For instance, in the example blessing below, taken from pages 5–6, I have removed the personal attribution "Holy One" and have—through the blessing—changed the *You* to *us* or *we*. Additionally, I have made the petitions calls to the community—*Keep us* becomes *May we be kept*, and *Remind us* becomes *May we be reminded*. In doing so, we turn the blessing inward, over the gathered community and individuals.

Blessing for a First Day

> May the power of love alone,
> hover your hand of blessing
> over us, on this first day—
> to make it rich with friendship and challenge,
> with joy that comes from knowing
> that our endeavors shape lives,
> futures, hopes, and dreams,
> and this lovely and fragile world.
>
> May we find our places and ways,
> belonging to each other.
> Open our minds to new ideas,
> keep our hearts for your best purposes,
> always seeking justice,
> and make of us the leaders our nations and peoples need.
>
> May we be kept from harm and sorrow,
> preserve us for everything good, kind, honorable, and joyous.
> May we be reminded that every challenge presents an
>   opportunity
> that every new friend invites a friendship with what is beautiful
> and every learning—in and out of the classroom—
> as a grace from love.

Let us rejoice then
in the wonders we are certain to behold
in the coming days
in these souls,
and in this community of strength, challenge, and care.

May we here become our best selves,
and find this to be our best way of giving thanks
for it all.

With open hearts we set our intention.

I hope and intend that these blessings offer options and inspiration for substitution and flexibility in naming and endings, and that the substance of the blessings will be sufficient to those who use this book, and will allow for variety in naming the spirit of our very diverse and varied communities. These blessings were originally intended and offered as oral forms. No one saw the page but me, so punctuation and capitalization mattered little. For publication, the *you* is lowercase for more versatility and to maintain a consistent style. You will know what your spirit, mind, and heart intends, and how to use and deliver such intentions to your campuses and those you bless.

You will, no doubt, find and write your own openings and may want to substitute them in these prayers, as fits your style, your needs, and your audience.

More attributions and opening phrases or names, are below, to stimulate your soul's imagination.

You might consult the 99 beautiful names of God from the Muslim canon, Jewish appellations for the Holy name, respectfully avoiding speaking the sacred Tetragrammaton. Or you might use Krishna, or other of the myriad descriptions of the faces and attributes of One who is within, listening and attentive to human beings as they call. I have enjoyed opportunities to create or invent new names and phrases, seeking new ways of understanding or describing the divine, the spirit, in relation to a community or individuals. Many of these attributions can be changed from God to Spirit. There are almost infinite ways to call to the best of our hopes, to place ourselves in the eye of One who transcends or inhabits us all.

> Source of all good
> Creative Spirit
> Holy one, tender and mighty
> Spirit who is the open door before us
> God, the threshold
> God of many names
> Holy One whose presence we honor
> God of yesterday, today, and tomorrow
> Changeless one, yet ever new
> Eternal Mother Lord
> Tender Source
> Creator Love
> Home of our souls
> Lifter of hearts and minds
> Oh Unifier of paradox, division, and polarity
> Holy One of many names and none and more.

> To the One whose name we utter in myriad ways:
> God
> Al Rahman Al Raheem
> Adonai Melech ha Olam
> Infinite love and beauty
> Lifeforce and source
> Nameless One
> One of many names and faces.

Many years ago, I offered the closing blessing on a meeting of Jewish, Muslim, and Christian leaders. A Christian lady confronted me afterward, scolded me, and inquired—in one of those questions that is really a statement—why I did not offer my prayer in the name of Jesus. Others have written theology on the matter to which I cannot do justice. I am a Christian—one who loves the rich diversity of others who love and follow God and wishes to include them in our public ceremonies and blessings. The name of Jesus, for me, is not a magic talisman that makes my prayers acceptable when other prayers might not be. Every prayer and every yearning of our individual and collective hearts is heard and known to the Holy One, who invites us to see ourselves in that auspicious light and love, and then to listen and watch for graces that answer our deepest longings.

.

Notes on Ending Prayers and Blessings

I think of these blessings as the lifting of our single souls and corporate hearts.

There are as many ways to end a prayer as to begin one. Many prefer "Amen," and I have done so often because our listeners, and even those who are not paying attention, know it means that the overtly spiritual time is concluded. Amen means "may it be so," which I have often used. Amen is used, in various languages and iterations, in Islam, Judaism, and Christianity (Ameen, Ah-mein, transliterating from Arabic and Hebrew).

Sometimes a particular ending means we will act on what is intended or suggested. Other times we invite a spirit or being to attend to our needs. Whatever you, or your community, know and think about what is taking place in blessings, they invite us to be open to something beyond ourselves, to ready our hands and hearts for receiving, to place ourselves in the care of another, or of each other.

I have rotated some possible endings in these prayers, though sometimes no particular ending phrase is also appropriate. The words themselves are not magic. We are inviting connection with ears, minds, and hearts. As with beginnings, you will find suitable phrases that mean "we are done" but that don't sound like parroting specific traditions. And sometimes sustaining the moment in silence or with no ending at all is the best option. I have done all of the above, and more, in these blessings.

You might substitute or include some of these or find your own way of ending a blessing.

This is our heart's desire
This we desire
Blessed be

May it be so
Let it be
This we ask
Peace
Please
With open hands and hearts
We will be/are grateful
Namaste

Blessings for
Your Students

Blessings for Transition and Change

Transition is inevitable on a college campus. It feels like ministry is a revolving door, sometimes with only one possible moment of touch or blessing for a student—this one right now. The academic life is endless circuits of beginnings and endings, overlapping coming and going while hardly knowing the difference, getting to know new people and saying goodbye to significant models and friends, grief and relief at once, hope and anguish, fear and courage. Some portion of the community is always leaving to go abroad, to graduate, or to transfer, and arriving from travels, summer work, time off, or death in the family. Students returning are transformed by their experiences. Students who have remained are in new relationships, thinking new ideas, seeing themselves in unexpected disciplines and vocations. Every semester, classes and friend groups are remade by the schedule, Greek life, athletic practice, and where students live. Each student is in constant flux in identity formation, spiritual seeking, and trying on ideas and identities, making continually new senses of themselves, their families, and their minds and hearts—through their learning that leads them in new directions and understandings. They investigate the riches of diversity beyond their expectations and learn to build bridges with others who are different from themselves. There may be no more fertile time than these traditionally 3–4 years.

The transition happening in young adults might be described metaphorically as wrestling, mining, panning for gold, planting and harvesting, journeying, mountain climbing, and even playing dress-up. The nature of identity formation and rapid changes invite the juxtaposition of ideas and playful images that highlight discontinuity and snag listeners' attention. Imbalance also characterizes moments of growth and realization, and I sometimes like to use ideas or words that are not exactly compatible in order to jar students and communities to greater mindfulness and waking presence. I have also noticed that on a college campus, the future is so often the focus of life, and we are so frequently looking forward that the now, the present state and time can be easily passed over, neglected, used as a stepping stone rather than mindfully experienced. For this reason, I often focus on one given moment of time, to remind us not to miss it.

Some campus transitions are highlighted in ritual functions, where the chaplains might bless the gathered. In cases of the outdoor rituals, the chaplain can be charged with praying that the weather holds, and it's good to harbor a sense of humor about this expectation. (The same goes for praying before football or other athletic contests.) Other transition rituals can be private, off the beaten track, uncomfortable, and without a romantic sheen or even a sense of their larger meaning. These private moments or experiences need blessing as much as the public university structures of transition. A wise eye perceives and takes part in change as challenge and blessing too.

Opening the Year
A New Beginning

May everything ordinary be sacred
on this most hopeful day.

May the crystal sky open to wisdom
and every garden's brilliance sing joy.
May elders step to leadership
and early souls be friends.

May careful planning yield shared vision,
moving to willingness,
and anxious anticipation find its own delight.

May trouble linger far and away,
every worry bring health and justice,
all days become new moons of forgiving grace.

May every act of compassion be a radiant blossom,
each word a pearl to discover and revere,
the richly blessed
be those who now must bless in turn.

And thus may each new day
be its own fresh origin
as we become our dearest and deepest best.

This is our desire.

For Those Who Go First

Be praised
for those who go first,
who lead the way,
try and fail and succeed,
create better for those who follow.

For their sacrifice and success,
for hearts and souls,
minds and bodies,
eyes, ears, hands, and feet,
we give thanks and follow.

Bless the journey now,
and be pleased to travel with them—
to be present all the way,
start to finish,
from this day and
for all the days to come.

Amen.

Blessing for a First Day

Holy One,
whose power is of love alone,
hover your hand of blessing
over us, on this first day—
to make it rich with friendship and challenge,
with joy that comes from knowing
that our endeavors shape lives,
futures, hopes and dreams,
and this lovely and fragile world.

May we find our places and ways,
belonging to each other.
Open our minds to new ideas,
keep our hearts for your best purposes,
always seeking justice,
and make of us the leaders our nations and peoples need.

Keep us from harm and sorrow,
preserve us for everything good, kind, honorable, and joyous.
Remind us that every challenge presents an opportunity,
that every new friend invites a friendship with you,
and every learning—in and out of the classroom—
as a grace from your hand.

Rejoice with us then
in the wonders we are certain to behold
in the coming days,
in these souls,
and in this community of strength, challenge, and care.

May we here become our best selves,
and find this to be our best way of giving thanks
for it all.

With open hearts we set our intention.

A New Year

Open our arms today
in happy hope that this will be a home,
a haven of learning and love,
where every part of us will be alive
to wonder, curiosity, awe.

In this welcome
make us know the wider embrace
of the great and holy Friend
whose name is love,
who lights our way,
illumines the truest questions,
and paves every future with promise and delight.

Open our hearts and minds
to new friends we will meet,
to mentors we have only longed for,
challenges not yet comprehended,
tastes of wisdoms we can only imagine,
and to spiritual and intellectual light
that will guide us all the way—
now and through the years,
that our lives and community may be
the service we gratefully offer
to this world in need.

Make it so then,
for us, and for us all.

Amen.

At the Gate of the Year

Infinite and Tender Friend,
for the new breath of morning
and the graces of this day,
for friends and travelers for the way,
we raise grateful thanks.

At the gate of the year
we bless:
the mixed routine and unfamiliar,
the boundlessly energized and the anxious unready,
the joyous and bereft,
those we have yet to know,
and those who will be heroes and mentors.

In your great mercy,
sweep us now
to risks of daring beauty,
to bounties undiscovered,
unimagined depths of mystery and justice
and joy we might not yet dream,
that the yearnings of our full and empty hearts
might become strength
to follow fully reasoned love to the brink.

Then in our common striving,
in every fluent or stuttered
act of hope—

hear the ageless resounding
of your own great name
in us.

A Vision for a New Class

Holy all-seeing and all-knowing One,
bless our eyes and hearts and minds.

Grace us with the sight of those who know what matters
    most—
in the close moment and in the long view—
with courage to pursue with persistence and vigor
the deepening paths we visualize
in your dreams for us.
Focus us for values of justice, dignity, kindness,
to improve and conserve the bountiful and ailing world
you have offered for our stewarding and joy.

Widen our vision
to perceive the humanity of those with whom we disagree,
and those who are different,
to make respect and inclusion our code for work and play,
that every challenge would be opportunity for growth
in the insights and boundaries of our hearts.

Help us see that we are better together,
that we need each other, that we are all flawed and
    wonderful,
and that every friendship is blessing,
and that love is a behavior.
Challenge us with guides and mentors
to discern any short-sightedness, and
correct our vision where it falters and misleads.

Show us that life is at once long and short,
a gift that matters every single day,
and may a depth of gratitude order our days
and inspire us to wholeness.

We seek vision and inspiration
to know your love for earth and all its inhabitants
that we may feel and act for those who suffer,
that we embrace transcendent and spiritual realities,
and know that we are deeply loved.

This is the prayer we offer for this new class,
and for all of us.

We Offer It All

Generous, Merciful—
bidden or unbidden,
from the beginning,
you are here and we belong to you.

We come as we are to you—
we bring our fear, anxiety, and uncertainty,
knowing that they are not hidden from your wise eye of love.
See and bless them all,
to birth from our emptiness and confusion
profound service, energy, and ability
we could never yet imagine.

Take, also, the miracles of our lives:
friendships, families,
minds that wrestle and ache and come to clarity,
the urge to freedom and care,
our efforts to correct burdens and create beauty.

We ask your blessing on our striving.
In all our hopes and dreams
make us people of grace,
that in every moment—both ordinary and momentous—
we may see your open heart
with ours,
and rejoice.

A Blessing of Blessings

We bless hellos and goodbyes,
parents, families, siblings.
We bless travel and settling,
books, backpacks, computers, phones,
rooms and residences,
friends, roommates, companions.

We bless guides, professors, and leaders,
rest, work, fun, study, and classes.
We bless syllabi, papers, labs, studios,
finances and budgets,
exercise and prayer,
smiles and tears,
searching and finding,
truth, failure, and discovery.

We bless success and disappointment,
holidays, sports, games, and every contest,
music, art, and doodling,
thinking, musing, profound Aha! moments,
small pleasures, happiness, and great joy.

We bless generosity, kindness, and understanding,
service and willingness to be served,
clubs and parties, hangouts, and snacks,
nourishment in kitchens near and far.

We bless bodies and bones, teeth, feet, brains, and faces.
We bless honesty, integrity, laughter, and struggle.
We bless souls, minds, and hearts.

Be blessed then, by all that is good and holy.
Be happy, productive, whole.
Be one of us—
the richly blessed
and those who must now bless in return.

Let it be so.

A First Day of Classes

Oh my soul,
what shall we say when our eyes flutter open
in the splendid clarity of early morning
and it's the first day of class
and we are more than ready but not yet ready?

Be praised, oh mercy, for the awesome gift of life
and for the courage we'll surely need for these days.

And what shall we say when we look about us
and perceive a realm of faces
for whom we do not yet have a name and story?

Be praised, oh friend, for the steadfast among us,
for the challenge and hope of new friends,
and for the risk, chaos, and blessing of community.

And, my soul, what shall we say when we lift our eyes to the
     hills
and our vision embraces stately scaffolds
giving way to pale brick and sparkling windows?

Be praised, oh creator,
for your presence in the double-edged gifts of history and
     progress,
for promise and memory,
and for carpets, cables, sidewalks, and paint.

And so, oh eternal one,
what shall we say?

Oh life!
Oh love!
Oh joy!

Amen.

Wrestling

Source of challenge and change,
we ask for blessing at the threshold of the year.

We already give thanks for
safe arrival, energy, and sense of humor,
for minds and souls and gifts,
for the people we are and will become.

Give us grace
to wrestle with wisdom
and befriend you, light and guide.
Offer your persistence and patience
through every thrill and disappointment,
every differing opinion and hope,
problem, and joy,
until we perceive its gift and claim its blessing.

Bless our coming in and our going out,
so to hold on for blessing
and find it all to be sacred
that every aspect of our lives—singly and together—
would sing your praise,
bless your Name,
and fill you with delight.

Blessed be.

For New Students

We make a blessing
for the gift of life,
for joy, for family,
and for the abundance
that brings us to this day.
We give thanks for students—
the hope they are and will be.

We ask blessings upon new students,
as they make friends and a home,
serving those in need,
caring for each other.
Give them patience, compassion, and joy
as they find and follow their sacred paths.
Bless them with strength of body, mind, and heart,
compassion, protection, wisdom,
and always love.

Let the blessings and gifts
of the divine heart
shine upon us all.
Multiply the work of ordinary human effort
that it may become extravagant and precious
and yield rich blessings
for us and for the world.

In it all
remind us that we are deeply loved,
that we may be at peace, happy, and whole.

This is our hearts' desire.

For the Fall

Heaven help us!
When August wanes and turns to fall
we remember own our awareness of
anxious shuddering joy
and tender yearning
for all that is before us,
ever more than we can manage,
yet to that which our hearts draw instinctively—
a blessing of tremulous hope.

We restive souls alight with readiness
and a bit of recoil too,
gather now in the shape we find ourselves,
open to what is and will be.
We face our common direction—
a community of friends,
diverse and whole,
seeking the inspiration due this moment
as we head toward who we might be or become.

Whatever hope or fear drives us now,
whatever calling compels each and all,
reach forward and open us
for the prize of the honorable work we do,
fine souls, ready partners,
humanity in need of what we have,
and more—in who we are.

So, we declare, ready or not,
we begin now,
for the world we embrace and love,
for those who are yet to come
into our common and uncommon life.

Heaven will help us.
No doubt.

At the Beginning,
We Make Three Turns

We give thanks for the productive summer
and the enriching gift of time.

We acknowledge the grief
of unfinished projects, undone plans,
what wasn't worth doing,
and dreams that want renewal.

And we turn forward
hoping to see the best of ourselves
in each other,
glimpsing our horizon
and setting face to reach it.

We need blessing in our endeavors
to be strong, clear, and wise,
to persist in the vision of the heights before us.

May we be true to our values,
to live with open hearts
as we learn, grow and change.
May we seek justice and equality,
telling the truth—
candid, courageous, and constructive—
making plans with humility and hope.

May we find ways to treasure each other,
this land, and the blessing of life itself.

Yes, please.

To Be Our Best

Our Community Hopes

Eternal—
you who in the beginning
bathed nothing with pulsing wing
and spoke a word
to call it to be
in the glance of love.

Hover over us now your spirit life
so to order us,
that the words we speak here
become realities we dream of being:
honor, peace, truth,
diverse, lovely, and one,
just and whole.

And so bid our community hopes
to praise you.

We Do Not Know the Way

We offer the tender awesome Spirit praise:
for the drippling dreamtime rain,
for the graying of the night,
the familiar rustle and screech of earth's morning songs,
for breath that seeped in and out like gift,
and for this day's new light—
what we know, who we are,
what is just, and what we do right.

Now, if we struggle for sight,
or when we cannot see the way,
then in that rich darkness
nurture us, we pray, in such wise and loving heart,
like seeds warmed,
waiting in fertile soil,
that when the fulness dawns,
we will be green and ready,
knowing all the while,
and unafraid,
which way was up and out,
how to grow and stand,
how to balance, lead, and serve.

To that bright day,
as to you,
teach our hearts and minds
to reach.

Lead us now.

Who We Want to Be

Still, we rest in sacred time:
minds, hearts, and bodies poised
to ask and receive,
our empty cupped hands
outstretched,
ready.

Bestow upon we who wait
a sure sense of your stirring
in deepened hearing,
empowered and bold action,
careful, responsive, and holy justice,
a tender yearning
for what matters most
and an effortless will
to do as you inspire.

So make us
able to see
your gracious hand
in all we do
and are.

This Moment Matters

We pray
as we know that we are here
with our feet on the floor,
in these chairs,
arms touching each other,
surrounded,
breathing, thinking, feeling,
breathing.

Let us know that this moment matters—
that life is collected and spent
in these small openings
between opportunities and obligations,
that who we are is who we need to be,
that the ordinary is blessed,
that sacred wisdom is plain as day,
and that all of it adds up to only this:
one moment
one place and community
one task before us
one breath, one thought
and just enough for the now.

Let it be, then.

To Perceive the Best

Thou of many names,
revealer of riches,
we invite your blessing.

We ask for joy and stubborn strength
to dig until we find the gold within us,
to grow until we are our best dreams,
and to keep ourselves open for gifts
yet to be extended and embraced.

Help us receive the riches offered
in joining a community of peers,
by letting sons and daughters go
and by giving our best to the work ahead.

Give us vision to perceive the bounty
in friends,
in learning that stirs us to action,
in ideas that sharpen our respect for each other,
and in the struggle to live for justice.

Help us understand the beauty of the struggle,
and the challenge, too, in what comes easy.
We open our hearts,
in trepidation, happiness, and gratitude,
knowing that we are already richly blessed.

With open hearts, Amen.

Open to the Unexpected

Source of life,
breath we welcome but do not control,
we offer thanks for this moment—
not as we expected nor wanted,
but as it is.

We ask for blessing:
give us grace to be and love and work and pray
where we are,
to find gratitude and hope here,
to seek deeply in our hearts for meaning and wisdom,
to welcome the surprising
and the unanticipated gifts in life,
even the unexpected.

May the spirit of love
bless our endeavors—
to be a safe and caring community,
to keep vital and strong our families and learning
    communities,
to guide our leadership with clarity and wisdom,
to shower us with compassion and hope,
in storm and peace,
and to lead us to shared vision and justice.

Surround us daily with the light of your divine love
that we may find new ways to be open,
to treasure each other

and the blessing of life itself,
in this moment
and the next
as it arrives.

This is our hearts' desire.

The Spirit of Endings
A Spirit of Ending

Spirit of the ancients
and of those who have gone before us,
may our gratitude be your praise
for the days that are past
but live cherished as memories
and treasures for mining.
Your strength has brought us through
and to this day rejoicing.

Spirit of the singing sparrows and warming sunlight,
may our pride do your heart sweet honor
as we give and receive the rewards of our labors.
Accept resounding thanks
for the glory of now, here, and what is.

Spirit of distance and motion,
of endless possibility,
be with us as we travel unfamiliar roads.
May truth and justice guide all our acts
and compassion temper our lives,
that we may blossom and become
our sweetest selves.
Include us now among those
happy to be travelers,
and grant us the comfort of knowing
that you move with us everywhere we go.

Spirit be praised.

Departures

Great divine guide,
we have followed as we knew
through failure and success
to this most joyous day.

Lead us now
again in this hour—
that our hearts would cross the divides
of grief and relief,
attachment and separation,
trepidation and courage.

Stay with us on the journey.
When we falter, encourage.
When we stumble, steady.
When we dance, laugh.
And help us become,
step by step,
more truly ourselves
for the world's delight.

May it be.

The Last Day and It's Cloudy

We weary and grateful pilgrims
acknowledge the Holy Eternal Thou
in the boisterous songs of birds,
in farewells and storms and promise,
in the faces of these fine souls gathered
to look upon your face and futures
in success and pride and narrow escape.

We admit to being ready and not yet ready
to take from this safe harbor
the gifts and skills and friends,
and to begin the journey anew,
to sojourn farther and again.

But oh Holy One,
lead on and we will follow.
Bring us to the land of fullest joy and gratitude.
Delight in laughter and tears,
and find honor by our lives.
and please, don't let it rain.

This we ask.

Move Over Our Time

Eternal Spirit,
who moved over the face of the waters
before even the first day,
and moves over our time—
we present you souls
like treasures gathered in pride, trepidation, and joy.

We acknowledge the miracles
of life, beauty, rain, wind,
the richness poured over us,
the grace in which we are kept.

Open us to your ways, Holy One,
that our being and doing may praise you
for all the surprising, ingenious ways you bless us.

Usher us travelers
into awesome worlds of fullness and joy,
as we laugh and weep,
go and come,
as we seek your presence
and your delighted face,
today and all the days to come.

Let it be so. Amen.

We Made It!

Let's just savor
that we have completed
a whole year
of joy and hardship,
hello and goodbye,
success and some failure,
loss and wonder,
the great revolving door of
campus seasons.

There's more to do—
moving, orientation planning,
reports, cleaning off the desk,
vacation.

But for right now
let's just be here—
happy, relieved, calm—
and celebrate that we have made it to today.

Welcome summer
Woohoo
Deep breath
Thank God
Alleluia
Amen

Commencement Blessing

Eternal Wisdom,
accept our grateful praise for the gift of this day,
for the blessings before us,
for our deep pride and hope,
for accomplishment,
persistence,
and success.

We ask your blessing
on these who graduate
into the callings prepared for them.
May their lives be bright and worthy,
and may their pursuits bring them honor.
May their lives serve humanity,
build enduring communities,
and may they have hearts to care
for this fragile earth that sustains us all.
May they reach out in hope,
through their own winters,
to bring warmth, joy, and success to others.

May we all know of your great and enduring love
through adversity and effort,
so that we journey from joy to joy,
as together we build and heal the world
you have entrusted to us in love.
Delight in our work and pride
as we laud and send these fine souls ahead

to do your work, in whatever place,
to live for justice and peace,
and to be their best selves.

May it be for your joy and your honor,
and by your blessing.

Travelers

God of distance and motion,
be with us now
as we travel this
unfamiliar way.

Give us the world's lights for our guides.
Give us inner light.
Give us your own light.
Give us a road
that takes us where we want to go,
where you desire us to be.

Lift our hearts beyond the loneliness
of strange vistas.
Keep us curious and invested
in what we may find around the next bend.
Calm any anxiety
over how we will be received
along the journey
and when at last we arrive.

Include us now among your people
who were happy to call themselves travelers,
and grant us the sense that you move with us
everywhere we go
and all the way.

Amen.

CHAPTER

2

Blessings for Challenge, Crisis, and Grief

There are those who claim that the college years are the best years of a life. This is true in many ways. They are also terrible years, marked by high emotion, moments that seem like failure, loss of all kinds, as well as imbalance, pretense, hard work that never seems to end, and nights that go on forever.

The chaplain's public work in a community is often to speak the silently obvious, to name the pain we feel singly or together, to say the things no one else wants to risk, even to articulate what is unmentionable in polite company—like injustice, worry, death, and even love.

Education is inherently based in risk: breaking, growing, changing, losing ideas and identities that no longer serve or fit, becoming someone new. We witness students transform during the university years, usually into adults we admire, capable, thoughtful, civil, and whole. The challenge can yield joyous results, and often does.

At the same time, students face increasing loss, the death of parents and friends, violence, rejection. The world is present in the university where gun violence, racism, homophobia, and every sort of prejudice, war, as well as natural and unnatural disasters impinge on our individual and collective hearts and minds. Even cancer is more prevalent on campuses than it was 40 years ago. And as parents delayed child-bearing, increasing numbers of university students grieve a long illness of a guardian or a sudden death in their immediate families. When a death occurs on campus or bereavement visits a member of a campus community, life goes on for the community surrounding them. Deep loneliness sets in when their world comes to an abrupt and painful halt, while colleagues and friends keep planning for and striding toward the future and their dreams.

Young adult communities are not shielded from loss and sorrow, and these are heightened by the identity formation losses that are already taking place, the shedding and replacing of identities, religions, genders, family structures, and even expectations. The effect of these challenges can be both devastating and another kind of opportunity to growth, a sense of what matters most, and the dangerous opportunities love creates in human life.

Not many universities still pray at faculty meetings, but faculty and staff—as well as students—need our prayer, our blessings, our summons to remember their sacred vocations, especially when times are hard. It is also the case for students that their exhaustion bears witnessing with honor as a normal part of the process of education.

Students' lives wax between dull, predictable, and wildly surprising events. Covid was one such abrupt challenge for students, faculty, and staff on every campus, when the cracks in the world were obvious. Deeply painful, it was also a generative time for some students who went home to their families, got to know their parents and siblings again, and spent unwilling but formative time learning to be in deep, honest, and grown-up relationship, as well as learning to learn in other contexts and modes, as was the case for faculty, staff, and administrators too. Over and over, making sense of the unpredictable, broken, even unsuccessful times is a subject of campus spiritual life, chaplains, and their prayers and blessings.

Feel free to add the name of the deceased or grieving where appropriate instead of pronouns I have substituted, or where you find (in this volume) an initial. Hearing the name of those who have died is a healing blessing. I always encourage emotions and tears—and claim them to be holy—in the face of a culture that takes a stoic perspective on "weaker" expressions like sadness and grief. If the chaplain's grief, real as it is, gets expressed, some might think you are not ok. This will be absolutely true. It is a matter of style for faculty, to decide how close to be with students, how much to feel for them. But it is the chaplain's job to care deeply enough about all students, all members of the community, that she or he is devastated when one suffers or dies.

Daily Challenges of Life
Fragile and Exhausted

We come as we are
with our passions and confusions,
hardly knowing whether we are coming or going,
knowing what we know and not knowing what we do not.
We are mortal, fallible, and prone to snark.

May our fragility
give us grace for this moment,
like the gift of the sun,
or moon, storm clouds arriving and passing.
May our deepest hearts be evident in our care now
and in our commitment to deeply hear others.

May our best selves surprise us
and may our willingness to learn make us better,
more vulnerable and open,
holy learners,
open, honest, who we are.

Let it be so now, for each of us and all of us together.

The Crush of Days

We are in the crush of days:
short for all our duty,
energy wan for its demand,
sunlight brilliant disappearing,
chills in ears and bones,
waning patience, humor, even awe.

Here, oh universe divine,
is what we need:
breath for grounding
respect in disagreement
clarity in muddle
lightness of wintery hearts
vision of the worthy struggle
focusing friendships
hope—or time—for rest.

Do bless us
with gratitude
soul freedom
and certain hope that this all matters,
now and in the days to come,
so that our very lives bless
in delight, joy, and even laughter.

This is our desire.

Seeking

Was it you
in the sweeping wind,
sheeting rain,
in the gradual light and brilliant blue,
in that curious unrest,
or in our finitude in the face of rawest power?

Is it you
reflected in our unique and familiar faces,
in recognition that we belong here,
to you, and to each other?
Was it you
in the drawing that led us here and now
into leadership and hope?

Is it you
in the wine's tang and aromas of friendship,
in rhythms of ice and laughter
in challenge, work, and growth?

Teach us to seek and see you
and to welcome you
as you welcome us.

Let it be, then.

Sleepless Night

Oh Sleepless One,
eyes wide, thrashing and worried,
not like you, we need rest, eyes to close, peace at night.

In the dark, we easily forget that you are there,
here,
in the low rumbles of breath,
in the vibration of the earth beneath,
in the hair-ruffling breeze.
We forget that yours is the world,
all hearts and minds,
including these anxious ones,
futures and pasts,
even cringe-worthy moments
belong to you, to your eternal wise calm heart.
We don't even know why we worry, frankly;
it benefits nothing.

So, will you hold these bundled worries,
take them into mighty and tender hands,
hold them for us until we need them again—
if we need them again—
until we need a pastime in the darkness?
Will you hold our hearts
and those we love,
and the future, mine, theirs, ours,
as we learn to leave it with you
at night and
in daylight?

In the dark night of Tuesday,
willingly offered, we feel your arms receive them,
and sense the unruffled Yes
that is your assurance.

So it is, then, we give it over to rest,
to trust, to sleep.

So it is.

Loneliness

Beloved,
you know when we are burdened and sad;
you know us, inside and out,
and love us.

Wrap your tender arms around us now
to hold us close in sorrow,
in this gaping emptiness,
in and around us.
Let your love be present here with us.

Remind us that your love is eternal,
that you will bring us into tomorrow
with your offer of daily joy.

Your love is enough
when we want and need more.
So sustain us here and now
in your own mercy,
as we are,
into as we shall be.

Discerning a Major

The whole world seems committed.
Friends know for sure
who they want to be
and what they want to do.
Majors declaring, adding minors.

Here, some of us are lost,
for whom too much is hard,
everything is interesting,
and nothing seems perfect.
What they wanted to love
is not it.
What their parents wanted
they do not.

Are you there?
Can you hear the struggle of mind and heart
that pushes and pulls,
hangs them over the abyss
of unknowing,
when everyone we know
is sure?
Can you see ahead
when we cannot?

Is there hope for our wandering souls,
to find their rest, their places,
their subject, ideas that love them back?

We know you cannot accomplish it for us,
but we seek a hint, a leaning,
a hope that we will know it soon,
that one stumble, one poem, one mentor,
one conversation, an equation
will uncover the way we are to go,
and a great relief will settle in.

Send your wisdom to help us know
that what we do will be a blessing,
that the major we choose will be a good one,
that we cannot go wrong,
and that it will all become plain.

And give patience for these restless hearts
as we wait, walk, work, and wrestle
for enlightening recognition
and a vision of who we are to be.

We ask with heart and mind
and with yearning wide and deep.

Panic

Things have gone wrong.
The world is on fire; there is war,
famine, homelessness, racism, danger.

We confess to feeling guilty
that our world has trouble too,
small though it be in the grand scheme.

Exams we are not ready for,
papers that don't write themselves,
friends annoyed at our distance,
our worry.
Others make it look easy,
but it's not.

Oh Spirit of power and rest, will we be able to do it all?
Can you give us strength enough
for the long nights and longer days?
Will our parents support our return?
Are our small minds enough?

Now we remember that last term
we came crawling
with the same questions,
and got through it then.

We will get through it now.

Please?

In Anxiety

Unfathomable mystery,
whom we know through the cracks in things,
we ask blessing
on the breaking open that hurts,
on the questions that propel us to investigation,
on the injustices that call us to work and prayer,
on the whispers of hope,
on the drive for integrity,
and the search for our wholeness.

Keep us on this side of fear.
May every seeking be for the sake of love.
May all answers be tempered by humility and grace,
and may every wisdom—in the face of the unpredicted—
bring us to awe.

Protect us—
in our restive and creative anxiety—
from desperation and resignation.
Give us joy in wonder.
Show us your hand in learning and teaching,
in our vision and surviving,
in every ordinary and extraordinary compassion,
and in the gratitude of knowing some small design in life,
in work
and in our dreams for better futures
for us all.

Race Discussions

Holy One,
Eternal justice,
be present here with us,
as we know you are,
always.
Also, we invite you.

Hold us in tender love,
as we see ourselves in the mirror of your will and love,
as we shudder
at our history,
facing our sinfulness
as Americans,
religious or not,
as selfish humanity,
those who easily look away and consider slavery another's
    problem.

Show us our hope and healing
day by day,
as we journey to see
and find your vision for lives
and for the one human race.

May we follow your daily invitation
into the path of love
and, thusly, honor you.

Let it be so.

Grief and Memorials

We Do Not Know the Way

This prayer was written a few days after the death of our
university president.

In times like these
we do not know how to ask
or what we need
or where to turn.

But this we know
to ask the Spirit, the Eternal—
who lives in every moment
and all at once—
to bless us now,
to hear from the silent spaces in our hearts,
to read between the lines of our knowledge,
to lead from within us,
in this hour, day, and year,
step by step,
steady, sweet, and sure.

Until we turn, looking back,
to recognize every happy accident of grace
with a simple claim—
Mercy, Alleluia.

Amen.

Remembering a Leader

Love, memory, and hope,
be present in our grief
as we give thanks for the gift of D.,
your willing servant and friend,
as we feel the sting of his absence
and the wide influence of his great love.

Hold all who love him
in the palm of your great hand.
Give us hearts to know that tears are born of love,
and joy wells from memory,
and hope from community.

Bind us up for the days ahead
that our lives may be brimming with hope
because of this friend,
because of grace,
because of life.

May it be, then.

In the Face of Death

Startled and alarmed,
a death in our midst
shocks us.

We are about the future—
planning ahead, shaping bright lives,
imagining all the way ahead of us.

Left to our own devices,
we might choose not to think of death,
yet here we are, in the unwelcome presence of mortality.

Wakened from complacency,
we see the fragile edges of life.
Reflecting on our legacies,
we wonder what will last.
Open to think of meaning,
we imagine who we have shaped.
And without this fine life, now,
we see the gift that is life,
which we wake daily to receive.

In gratitude we think
of our lives,
of opportunities to think about what matters most,
and perchance to reorder,
of choices that have meaning,
of awareness that love and care we spend affects others

more than we know,
of knowledge that breath comes to us as blessing,
with all the gifts of life itself.

So, we assemble in grateful hope
for long, happy, and productive lives,
love to share,
courage to change and grow,
and for freedom that comes from profound gratitude.

Let this be for us.

Memorial for a Colleague

Giver of life, inspiration of love,
and light in darkness,
we give you greatest thanks for G.,
for the kindness she freely bestowed among us,
for her wit and vigor, even to the last,
for the privilege of living, laughing, and working beside her.

We offer gratitude for the fulness of her life,
for undaunted tackling of challenges,
facing them down, resisting defeat,
even as we give thanks that her final challenge is over
and that she rejoices in reunion and peace.

We remember the ways she created order
with people and paper,
frustrated students and colleagues,
holding it all together
with calm precision and grace.

We see before us the love she nurtured,
her generosity of heart which made her dear to so many over
   the world,
and to us.
We recognize the power of her faith
that sustained her among us.
For all of these, and the infinite ways she touched and moved
   and improved us,
we praise the one who made, empowered, and instructed her.

Now we ask again for the mercies of your love,
for we who learn to live without her.
Sustain us in our loss and sadness.
Be for us all strength, comfort, and meaning
and reap in us the gifts of gratitude
at the privilege of knowing her,
and at every remembrance.

You, whose arms embrace our G.
as tenderly as any mother,
hold us too
and, in good time, give us back to joy.

Teach us, even in the face of death,
to treat each other gently
and to search in every face, moment, and friendship
for rare and precious graces.

May it be. Amen.

Death of a Friend

We know that in love,
everything in our hearts is clear to you,
acceptable,
welcome,
and that you are mercy in our need.

Your gifts are beyond our wildest possible imaginings,
your blessings rich beyond measure,
and our thanks rise to you
for the life of S.—
daughter, sister, friend.

Her short life was long and wide,
in gifts, in friends, in dreams and hopes,
in ways she opened us to the world
and challenged us to higher love and holiness
through her eyes and heart,
to others
and to you.

Praises be for her mind, for the clarity of her vision,
for dreams come true already,
for her beauty, inside and out,
for her love of people, her voice and song,
for her sense of humor, and the peace with which she lived.

You alone could have created such a wonder,
such a gift.
She belongs in completeness to you.

Teach us to be patient and gentle
with ourselves and each other
as we grieve.

Draw us together in our sorrow, in our hearts.
Enfold all who grieve her in your love,
comfort in fear,
honor grief,
and keep us safe in love
all the days of our lives.

Amen.

Gratitude in the Face of Death

Eternal One of ageless years,
Creator and Author of every day,
of life and breath itself,
accept our praise now
for the long and splendid life
of your beloved M.

We stand
in honor and respect of her life of great reach,
and render thanks
for all she has touched, transformed,
blessed, gentled, and blessed.

Remind us this day
that your wonders never cease
as we celebrate a wonder—
for wisdom and intelligence,
for the range of her service, honor,
for her stories, and those who love her,
and all the gifts she shared.

Grant her, in turn, the gift of peace
of mind and heart
that her life would continue
to bless us.

We make this prayer
and give our prayer
to the glory of the One she loved.

Let it be so. Amen.

Death of a President

"Death is not extinguishing the light; it is putting out the
lamp because dawn has come."

—Rabindranath Tagore

Holy Eternal Brightness of Being,
accept thanksgiving and honor for the life of N.
who brightens now the realms of light.

We see in wonder
that you give not suffering but life,
that tears are born of love.
Do not seal her absence from us, but preserve it,
to keep alive our bonds in the shape of N.'s presence
in heart, mind, memory, and hope.

We knew you in this luminous soul,
a visionary who lit our lives
with visible fire and vision,
in affection and respect,
stylish, intellectual and humored pursuit.
We praise you for presence and friendship
for all the ways she raised our heads and hearts—
for her trust in us and laughter,
for welcoming lights burning late,
for her brilliant caring for people, justice, and women,
the grace of her bearing and beauty,
at work and at play.
Our gratitude rises for her strength—

in adversity, in sickness, in love, in struggle;
for her decisive tender admonition and hope.
In remembrance and honor,
may we burn with passion
to be ever better, nobler, and more beautiful.

Free us from regret and shrinking, turn us to truth in courage
    and kindness,
enlighten our sure security, even in anxious and uncertain
    hearts.

Sweet and Holy Fire, bring mercy and love for deep grief,
brighter days, joy and hope,
a certainty that every soul is a rare and precious treasure.
Be praised in sun and fire, light and life, in death, darkness,
    and dawn.

May it be.

Death of a Student after Illness

Oh Eternal Spirit, your love never ends.
You give us love for our families and friends,
you sustain us in life.
Yours is the gift of tears from the experience and heart of
    love.

We give you thanks for the life of our friend B.,
    for the strength of her heart and soul
    for her anger at injustice compelling her to be educated and
        free,
    for her irreverence and wit, adventuresome spirit
    and drive for experience.
We thank you for her mind,
    for the fire which drew many to her
    and burned some of them.
We thank you for all the moments in which
    she overcame obstacles, survived the odds, toughed it out.

We know her as your offspring,
    created of your love,
    and, now that she is beyond suffering,
    whole, and at rest.

We pray to you in our need,
    and for all who mourn with us this day
    in this sudden bewilderment,
    especially for her family.
Where grief is complicated, remorseful, or unacknowledged,

grant freedom, tears, and community.
Give to us all light and the courage to love,
whatever the cost, even the pain and sorrow of loss.

Our lives are better because we knew and loved her.
Her memory will be heavy and hard,
blessed and light.
May her life live on in ours,
be held in our gaze and heart,
in living for justice,
in every challenge and joy.

You first gave her to us,
and we remain grateful.
We raise our hearts in affirmation
through every brush with death
that you are love eternal,
that love never dies,
that we, and B., are precious to you
and that even complicated friendship is a grace.

Receive our open hearts, as our laughter and our tears.

We Lay Open Our Hearts

We lay open our hearts before
the one who made and loves us,
these empty and sorrowing hearts
in which now we have a hole
the size and shape of our friend J.

We confess helplessness and anger;
we are bewildered and astonished
that one person's life
could touch this many,
and whose sudden death
could hurt this much.

Listen now, oh Creator,
as we render our stories of his life
as we cry and laugh, as we feel his touch on our souls, even in
    absence.
Be grateful with us for his gifts and friendships,
for those he influenced unaware,
for those still wishing to know him.

As life around us continues,
hold with us now in this small quiet moment,
as we remember
recall
recreate
the joy of his presence,
the shape of his face,

the sound of his laughter in us,
the recollection of the ways he loved us.
Make our grief and tears holy,
a way of remembering
and holding him close.

And then hold us for all our days
in grateful praise
for his light in our lives.
May his memory eternally bless us
and you.

Please let this be so.

Sorrow

Spirit of our dreaming,
you know our hearts and minds,
the futures we had imagined and desired,
even begun.

Some call you
Destroyer of Worlds—
an apt description, dare we say.
Well done, then,
death has destroyed life,
devastating ours.

Some say that you took our friend,
made an angel,
enacted your unfathomable and mysterious will.
And how
can we love you,
if this be true?

How will we continue
in sorrow?

Will you be called
holder of our broken hearts,
lover of the lost,
hearer of agony,
restorer, and sometime Friend?

We offer the truth of our hurt
to ourselves and to you.
And someday soon
may we call you Tender Love,
the One who wept before we knew,
who hovers over and around
in inscrutable silence?

3

Blessings for Justice

More students than ever participate in service opportunities on campus as part of their educational and co-curricular experience, as part of their commitment to the world and all of those who inhabit it with them. This engenders double gratitude on my part, as most of those service offices at universities grew from chaplain's offices and initiatives.

It is my experience that it is a sign of our success as educators when students turn their critical thought to making their universities—that have challenged and sheltered them—better, more inclusive and just. Over the decades of my own career, these justice issues have changed or have moved in cycles, as we learn more about our world and the causes and nature of injustice. Many justice movements make progress, or even begin, on university campuses. Whatever the issue at hand, chaplains can bless the protests by their presence, by words they speak, and they are often called upon to assist in the creation of these movements.

Other times, it is the nature of chaplaincy to "speak truth to power," to articulate injustice before it is widely perceived. We may raise specific issues in private meetings with senior leaders and also raise them in our blessings. Whatever the specific issues of the day, or of the university setting, our prayers draw together a sense of concern for those who suffer, who lack the resources to enroll or excel, and a sense of social issues that impinge on the creation and human communities—like gun violence, global climate change, racial inequity, war, religious exclusion, and an overwhelming list of more hurt and injustice. We also, and often, bless the difficult processes of dialogue and struggle that are inevitable in the face of conflict or change.

For Those Who Live Justly
For Healers

Holy Creator,
bless us now for those who follow you
in healing sciences and arts.

May their hearts be open to suffering,
to compassion as response,
to the possibility of hope and wholeness for all.

Make their hands gentle and strong,
their minds clear and capable,
and guide their words for life, blessing, and peace
to be like yours.

May friendship keep them strong,
your spirit give them awe
for the majesty of the human creation.

May their humanity be a blessing to you
in service of those you love
from the first to the last day.

And, in return, may our lives—
our work and hearts, bodies and souls, leisure and
    commitment—
give you blessing and joy.

Keep us in your grace
now and in all the days to come.

May it be so. Amen.

For Those Who Serve

Eternal and Wise One,
be praised for our life, health, and joy.
We invite your presence with us, always,
as we laud and honor,
give thanks
and swell with pride.

Guard these, now, with your hand and spirit.
Keep them in your path,
illumined by integrity, balance, and love.
Strengthen them
to be beacons of justice,
to affect our world
from greed to service,
disdain to understanding,
division to community,
and on into joy.

Praises be for those who have seen them along the arduous
    journey
to this moment of fulfillment and joy.

Be present now
as we send forth these gifts
toward the hope for reconciliation
for the building and healing

of this world you have entrusted to us
and that you love.

May your great heart find delight
and may it be to your praise and honor. Amen.

For Those Who Bring Good

Grateful we are to you,
oh God of justice and wisdom,
for life both fierce and frail,
for strength of soul and body,
for a moment of celebration,
and a deep breath.

Bless us now,
that our lives bring good to this desperate world,
always moving to equity and peace,
as agents of inclusion,
advocates for the voiceless,
sources of joy.

Make us ready for what is before us,
with courage for this great calling,
with grace and gratitude
to be friends, at all times, for you.

May it be so. Amen.

Scarcity

In a Lenten world
where markets plunge,
assets shrink, people worry,
and even groundhogs fear shadows,
show us the meaning of the looming scarcity.

If we shift with ebbing tides,
root us in careful hope.
When we grasp for safety,
push us to daring inventiveness.
If drawn to sacrifice,
deepen our hearts to discover riches
beneath our feet.
When we fear the future,
show us strengths untapped.
When we pull away,
wrap us in the bonds of living communions.
And at any sign of despair,
draw us back into your holy lap of love.

Thus, in every moment of less,
teach us the more
of what matters most,
that our hope be full,
our faith be thoughtful,
that our treasures be
shaped like justice, caring,
and love.

So do we ask that you sustain and keep us
that we might discover,
celebrate, and delight in
the abundance of your heart's grace
in us.

May Wisdom Light Our Way

Divine Wisdom,
as the moon lit the evening
to help us know our way,
so now light our path this day
as unmistakable and true.

As morning frost blanketed the ground
twinkling in the growing light,
so cover and surround us
to make us also wonders
in your service,
sure, unafraid, strong, blessed, and just.

As breath graced our morning waking,
so grant us now to understand
the graces we are poised to discover,
know, and share.

Now and always,
may our lives give praise.

In Praise of Giving

Generous Heart
whose full wonder
first inspired
words of creation and acts of love.

We invite the honor of your Presence
in sign and wonder and grace.

Be praised in passionate giving,
in lives reflecting
eternal circles of compassion,
received and returned
as mercy and gift.

May we see your heart once more
applauded, modeled, moved,
inspired in us all again
to love kindness, do mercy,
and to walk in the humility of awe.

May it be so for us. Amen.

That We May Do Justice

A Prayer for Justice

Holy and Infinite Love,
in this world of injury and disaster,
in uncertain days,
in the worries of this one moment,
we confess our great need.
Our pale attempts to change
and make justice from the shreds of what once seemed
    wondrous
bring us to sorrow.

Give us compassion and generosity for those
whose anguish is deep and wide,
whose loss is unfathomable.
Break our hearts until we know that we belong to each other,
until we become the humanity you created and meant us
    to be.

Make our minds and backs strong for the work we must do,
apart and together:
to understand and love the different,
to create more peace than conflict,
and to save our earth, our children,
and each other.
May our ancient hatreds be silenced by the justice
for which you call and equip.

Inspire, teach, and lead us
that in the riches of the Spirit's grace
we may rise in grateful service
with lives that benefit others
and praise the author whose name is Love.

May it be so. Amen.

Blessing for a Comedian

If we laugh today,
then let it be grateful recognition of truth no one else will tell,
medicine for souls, overflowing blessing,
cleansing refreshment,
and brilliant opposition to any dreary day or thought.

If we weep today,
let it be for all injustice—
thoughtless bigotry diminishing our common humanity,
for a selfish vision that narrows the world to just me.
While humans and nations suffer unbearable strife,
or at least for the terrified, hopeless, and broken,
may tears be prayers
for freedom,
food,
peace,
wisdom.

And if we laugh ourselves to tears
over the other's flaw or bemusing inconsistency,
then may all cosmic creative chortling energies and ironies,
make it cleansing blessing:
lives mirrored by poking fun to critical challenge,
rousing the idle to action,
widening our ways to live and move,
in healing, hope, and joy
for this broken, tender, and sometimes hilarious world.

So let the laughter well up in us,
deep, transforming, and holy,
and let it rise to your listening heart.

May it be so. Amen.

We Work on Ourselves

Oh greatest hope,
we are in it together,
that much is clear.
So, we give thanks for this community,
for the intentional and gritty work
of becoming who we most want to be
and who we best will become in common.
Accept our thanks
even before we fully intend it,
as we live toward
and into our highest hopes.

Give us grace to remember
to try
to allow heart and minds space
to see good and truth in those
with whom we disagree
and whom we may dislike.

Fashion us into a unity
built of respect,
if not agreement,
owned by hope and grace.
And make of us the gift
we will be together,
even now in this place and time.

May our manner of life
become our greatest praise.

This we desire.

Conflict

Give us hearts and minds
to share in the joy
and grief
of those around us,
to see life from many views,
to feel the impact.
Give us ears to hear what others say and mean,
give us voice to consider our own welfare
tied to that of all those sitting, working, living around us.
Give us patience to persist,
to enter transforming dialogues we would rather not entertain.
Give us hope to seek to be better people, better community,
and to want what it takes to get us there.

In the meantime,
we seek strength for our work,
our times,
our burdens and longevity.
We ask humility, wisdom,
and the knowledge that we are in the right place
and the right time.

In it all,
we ask for blessing, for inclusion,
for real and deep talk—profound and transforming—
and the sense that we make a difference
by what we do and by who we are.

Let it be so.

Erase the Contradictions

Poet Spirit,
All-Seeing One,
by our invitation now,
discern us as we are
with your heart of grace.
Perceive us too as we might be,
as we will be under your protective and progressive nurturing.

Where there is distance, bring us toward you, toward our
     awakening.

Give us eyes and hearts
to clearly see and know those we teach and serve,
to nourish them forward into their best selves.

Be with and in us now,
in what we do
and in who we are,
that there be no contradiction,
no separation,
and that we will be a more true
reflection of the great unity of you.

Was It You?

Did you
gust through our trees and hair,
rolling trash lids down the hill?

Do you beam out in infinite stars
and brilliant sun?
And was it to you
we abandoned our cares to sleep
and, waking, found ourselves
held, guarded, and restored?

Do you call us to greater caring,
empowering justice,
and a love that really matters?

And will it be you to lead us
in all the vexing questions
that claim our minds and hearts
with that same humor, brilliance, and care
that moves us to do and be our level best
knowing that in you
nothing is ever wasted?

Now in faith we know
that it is you to whom we lift eyes and souls,
that you have prepared us for this day,
these tasks,
these friends,

this world,
and for your glory.

May it be so. Amen.

Lives Meant for Service

We have so much to be grateful for—
breath in the morning,
the ability to think, move, and work;
sustaining health,
family to love,
friends that inspire,
even critics to insist we grow,
and a history of transformation.

And so much we could still ask—
for capacity to praise for all the good,
for the will never to take for granted,
hearts to seek after justice for all and each,
the drive to be better, do better,
to rise to every challenge,
the desire to draw closer to an ideal
of who we want to be,
and for our hopes in fruition,
for time to rejoice in achievement,
rest in trust that all is well,
clarity to know that we are more
than all our doings,
and that each of us is precious to the eternal.

In it all,
keep us mindful
that our lives are meant as service
to those not so blessed,

and may our best efforts
make this world a safer, better, more whole
reflection of your desire and intention.

Make it so, in our joy and in our striving.

Nudge Us to Justice

Tender Friend,
do bide your sweet time with us
as before, and more.

Walk with us, and make us willing
to do your bidding.

Hear us to vision,
lead us to our own honest success,
support us to strength of character and common life,
partner us to progress,
nudge us to justice,
and love us into joy,
that our ways might be only yours,
and that your ways show brightly in us
to the honor of all that is true
and enlightened
and full of hope.

We Greet Life with Awe

We greet life with awe
that it is so ordinary and yet full of import,
so daily and ultimate,
and that it is the gift of ourselves all day long.

Turn us to clarity
to know the meaning of our existence
in hope and trust
that we might make a real difference
in this lovely and dangerous world.
Bring a longing for peace
that gives way to action and belief.
Open grace to know and choose the best,
the wisest and most true
actions, passions, callings, and dreams
that what we say and what we do
might be one great trajectory
that makes the universe sing.

Thus may we waste not one moment
of this great responsibility and gift
that lies within and before us.

4

Blessings of Wonder and Hope

Much of the academic enterprise can seem disembodied—brain work, heady conversations, deep thought—or at least it can look and feel that way to those on the outside. Current students value their physical health, and the gym is widely used, much more than spaces of prayer, meditation, and silence.

Many of these prayers and blessing call attention to physical beauty and the world around us, which—despite the special care to provide these beautiful spaces—may be largely unnoticed as we go through days that are busy, our minds elsewhere, our plans far in the future, our concerns swirling deep within our hearts and souls.

I have invited students, and others, to focus on what is in front of their faces, even in their lungs and noses, inviting gratitude for the gift of life which may be overlooked or taken for granted. A more embodied approach to our spaces, noticing the beauty around us—seasons, stars, the myriad colors of green—is a discipline of great importance transcending the confines of religious division and self-importance. As we train students to think, we can also teach them to see, notice, and sustain a sense of wonder in the world, in themselves and each other, in their learning and growth, and in the disciplines they study. Wonder is a spiritual awe that keeps us—in equal parts—grounded and in tune with transcendence. It is a practice of mindfulness, noticing what is right in front of our noses, in our relationships, in family, in classes, and everywhere if we choose to look and see deeply, with spiritual eyes. Wonder can also be imitated and inspired. Our students need to see and hear their mentors in states of wonder, which will also make learning easier, more fun, and more exciting.

I often am inspired by nature, by the changing seasons, by wind, moon, as evidenced by these prayers.

Anything can be a wonder—from the tiniest detail to the most enormous patterns of the universe.

Hope is also a wonder and a result of wonder. More and more of our students have limited hope—for the earth, for the value of their education, for their parents' and guardians' wisdom, for their own ability to excel in life. We need to ask for and seek hope, embody its values, pursue it, and name it every time we can. I include hope here, in wonder, because they live together.

Open to Every Wonder
We Ask to Be Open

We begin with a blessing.

A blessing is an invitation to all that is holy to be with us,
to inhabit and shelter our abundance and need,
a welcome to the Spirit of life to be upon us,
to prepare and honor us,
to make more of what already is,
to fashion something from our less,
a giving over of what we expect,
a welcome of what will be,
and a door into the unimagined.

A blessing is an opening in us
for hope, direction, meaning.
It is a moment of awareness
that we are not alone
and that we live
at liminal edges of discovery.

A blessing is a prayer
offering who we are and what we have,
a willingness and intention to be useful and used,
a collection of hearts and minds,
summoning the best of ourselves
for others.

Blessed be, then.

Hope in Darkness

In the season of darkness and light,
a time of stark contrasts and discernment,
in short days and long nights,
we seek light.
We long for it.

In poignant and long shadows,
in longing and waiting,
we seek our own source of light,
to further understand the character
of what we do and who we are,
to distinguish what constitutes justice
and our particular callings to make illumination possible.
And we learn the origins of our hope.

Hope receives.
It holds out open hands.
It persists in and through us.
We invite it to appear
in our hearts and lives,
in our community,
and in our world.

Let it be.

Welcome Wisdom

May the wisdom of ages
dwell among and in us
as host and guest.
Guide, inspire,
and charge our pursuits
that we may find what we seek,
become living words of hope,
wonder at blessing
for ourselves,
for others in our midst,
for those we love,
and those we serve.

Namaste. Peace. Amen.

Fiery Mercy

Source of fiery and tender mercy,
be honored in this and every moment's mystery.

Accept our praise for sun and downpour.
Blow now a wind in our midst
that we may know the flames of passion,
the warmth of love,
and the heat of dreams.

Accept our lives as gifts
to our fragile world.
May they become honor
for the author,
bread for the children,
and living sprites of grace.

Bless and keep us.
Reside in the spaces between us
and sustain us ever friends.

May our proud hopes
be your honor
and may you be praised in our living.

This we desire,
and to it we commit.

Sharing Multiplied Loaves

Blessed One—
we know and welcome your presence
in the grace of maple's blaze,
in fellowship and commitment,
in duty, service, and joy.

You blessed loaves and fishes
and fed multitudes.
Come to us and bless the offerings
we are and make.
Multiply among us what we need and share.
Create in us not just enough to go around
but abundantly more
in blessed excess.

Eternal One,
as you hovered over chaos,
do now abide in and among us
to shape and form us in beauty and service.
Create here wisdom, clarity, direction, harmony
as we have not yet known or dreamed.

We offer ourselves to your blessing
all we are and will be, all we have and desire,
that the fragments of our brokenness, like bread,
feed souls and bodies,
and that our healing might sing
and be the whisper of your praise.

The Ones on Whom We Stand

Ancient of days, lives, and dreams,
in whose arms the wilds and tenders of eternity rest,
lift up all those who love you, this day,
by sacred remembrance,
honorable hope,
and the presence of delight.

The span of moments we remember and bless
sing glory, honor, joy
to the ones on whom we stand,
who established and built,
who live before us and together in your knowing.
Yesterday's vision of justice returns to us,
calling for all futures
bound up in perpetual movement,
at once now, and tomorrow.

Holy Beloved,
from sacred time and space,
send us onward,
brave enough for compassion,
with mercy sufficient to progress,
and with hearts full of wisdom's gratitude.

And peace.

Eternal Wonder

Eternal Wonder,
we slept while your vital moon
stood watching guard
casting crystals at the tips of every grass blade.

We rose to greet the joy and duty of day
and you recreated the morning, the breath,
the deepening hues of leaves and earth and sky.

We awe at your gifts, extravagant graces for joy alone,
that accompany the very life we enjoy—
enough and more of everything good.

We bring you a gift today!
Our souls and eyes and hearts and arms,
minds and wills,
our separate and common passions and callings,
our energy and drive and yearning.
We offer our best treasures
that in depths of united insight,
inventive wisdoms, and hopeful curiosity,
all the experience brought to this one day,
you may be seen—close and loved.

Now watch, enlighten, inspire,
shape these wonders
to become instruments
of blessings,
bright, holy, strong.

Do this not for our amazement
but for your own wise pleasure,
that all we do and have and are
might give back our thanks.

Let this be.

Football and Family

Oh Holy Delight—
for the beauty of sun and fall warmth of this day,
for the teams and our universities,
the preparation and performance,
for gathered friends and generations,
enthusiastic fans,
for competition, effort and cooperation,
for music, cheers, food, and fun—

We are grateful and happy.

We ask for goodwill and grace,
for good times and safety from any harm,
for fairness and civility,
and for an afternoon of adventure,
basking in joy,
ours and yours.

Be with us and bless us, we pray.

Amen.

For This One Student

A student with whom I had listened and companioned often about her identity and faith, her vocation, and her friendships, asked me to write her a blessing as she prepared to graduate and move away, and she reports that she has this prayer taped to her mirror.

Holy and Tender One,
bless this lovely gift of yours, E.

Thank you for her life,
for who she is in all lovely fulness and complexity—
for her abilities and challenges
and for the questions she has asked and will,
for her growing faith in the you she has come to know as
    friend,
for the tending of hurts,
for her own mind and heart whose trust is hard-won and
    resilient,
for her friends, hard work, and hope.

For the future daily nearing—
make her ready for it all.
Be visible among friends she chooses.
Be known in her success.
Tangle up your love in the family she creates
and may every meaning she makes include your abiding
    belief in her.
Extend your blessing as she commits to her part to make a
    more just world.

Protect her from every evil and make her graceful in the face
    of hurt.

May her heart always know
your delight in her, as she is, as she will be.
Open daily your hand and heart
to shower her with every blessing, strength, and courage,
and make of her life a radiance in which everything good is
    transparent
and real.

And may holy friendship between us—her and me—
keep our love in great joy
for all the days to come.

The Great Name name be praised, for you, E.

Friendship

Was it sufficient
that we drew deep breaths
and relished the scents of spring—
of leaf and flower—
and raised our faces to the sun
and breeze
and noted, for but a moment, the gifts of the universe?

Would it be enough if we looked around us today,
and noticed our friends,
whose lives matter in every way,
our pride, the hope
of those who know us well
and who love, support, and believe in us,
beyond what we can do for ourselves.

It is enough
to be together,
to laugh,
to receive blessing—
the gift,
and a hint of the way forward.

Thanks, then, we say.
Thanks.

In Our Foolishness

Laughing One,
remind us of foolishness.

Some days our spiritualities appear foolish:
bowing before an altar or image,
asking for help before getting out of bed,
putting our heads on the floor,
digging in dirt,
meditating on emptiness,
giving thanks for challenge,
following what we cannot see.

We yearn for the day
we see clearly what matters,
knowing with certainty,
grasping even the gifts of death.

So, in the meantime,
we seek wisdom
to live in humility,
to confess what we know,
to embrace without shame what we do not know,
to waste a little time
and care more.

In a moment of rush
it may seem foolish
to take a moment to breathe,

to write a poem, call a friend, light a candle, hum a tune.
Even so, we ask for strength and grace
to embrace the wisdom of the foolish
and to believe that what we do makes a difference
in our small circles, and this needy world.

Let it be, then.

Natural Wonders

A Solar Eclipse

Source of sun and moon,
you bless us daily with the gift of life, abundance, and joy.
you invite us to be light in the world,
friends of those who seek a transforming culture
that offers meaning for this present moment of division
and hope for our collective future.

Bless us this day
as we seek your signs in the heavens
that we see every shadow as a fertile harbor
where we may collect and reorder priorities.
May we seek in every sun's ray
your blessing and protection,
the heft and delight of your calling on us all
and the chance for right and light to shine through us.

Now let there be no eclipse in our kindness, in learning to
    love,
or in our commitment to justice
for the whole human family
and for our community,
now ready to serve in gratitude and hope.

Let it be.

The Wonders of Science

Everywhere we look we see wonders:
the sun, moon, stars,
this day's warmth and beauty,
the redbuds bursting forth in lushest purple,
infinite shades of green to dazzle the eyes.
Even the tiny drifts of blowing pollen call us to attention,
to mindful participation in this world,
in this precious commodity called today, this hour, this
    moment.

Thanks for those who lift our eyes,
for mystics, artists, and scientists
who call us to see distant horizons
and draw our sights high and wide
to perceive wonders of which we are not yet aware,
to understand responsibilities we have not yet accepted,
who call us to steward more carefully
this earth and sky and home and life.

Now, keep us in wonder
even in a hectic time,
to the awe that planets spin,
grass grows, the wind blows,
and the infinite is somehow present with us here
in the fragility and fullness of it all.

And may we live well every tiny and enormous detail
of this marvelous life

with thanksgiving, care, and praise,
so our very lives, singly and together,
become our call to action and our song of hope.

For the Wonder of Music

Oh Thou of swirling stars and wind and voices,
you, in the miracles of luminated sky
and the humbling tones of earth,
in the harmonies of face and soul:
our hearts lift in longing for the breath—
the soaring sound that is your delight among us.

We thank you for the song that is ours,
transported from the beginning,
by those who heard the ringing of justice,
the poetry of thought, spirit, love,
until we now follow its rhythm
through glory
through dimmest challenge,
through mystery, through every open way
and into spaces of purest wonder,
that you compose for us in tender hope.

Hear and accept our hymns and hearts of honor,
that our life may be in
ceaseless voice
one sweet and endless
melody of praise.

May it be, then.

Between an Earthquake and a Hurricane

This prayer was offered between the end of an earthquake and the beginning of a hurricane, literally, one day apart. It brought to mind the quality of prophets coming with divine signals and symbols, another example of using nature to inspire us to prayer.

Let all the blessings and gifts of this place
rain down upon you,
shower you with beauty, friendship, grace.
Let all thunder be joyous expressions
of energy, ideas, and true reflections of your own joy.
And may all the shakings come from the deep power
of your souls
and the spreading hope of your bright lives
as you find your sacred path and your heart's home.

Be at peace, then, blessed, happy, and whole.

Let it be.

Spring Praise

All thanks we offer to the Artist
whose word and spirit authored
all the spring-ish shades of green,
whose breath in us rose to morning,
and whose heart is bent toward earth.
All praise!

We submit now to that same wisdom,
the ageless eternal wonder.
We give ourselves, now, again, to you,
in hope and trust, for deliverance and guidance.

May our sight be clear
and our purpose true and eager,
to serve the causes of right and justice,
learning, growth, high calling.

Do now inspire us to new hopes
for ancient and sure dreams.
In all, may our thriving,
our living,
bring you honor and delight.

Be praised in these blue-green vales,
And in these gracious lives.

So may it be. Amen.

Breath

A deep breath can change the world.

It claims our space in the world.
It makes us large and strong.
It connects the hemispheres of our brains,
unifying our forces for good.

One breath brings energy—ground up—
into our souls,
connecting heaven and earth,
binding us up into a whole.

An inhale permits compassion
to transcend fight, flight, and passivity.

An exhale cleanses.
It is a holy, sacred gift.

A breath remind us
that, hard as we try,
we do not control the world,
or life,
that the wind of life is given by the moment
and we are both dependent and of eternal value.

A breath reminds us our humanity,
that no amount of doing
can make us more or less
a delight to the universe.

If the fluttering of butterfly wings
can change weather patterns,
then so can a calmly drawn,
slowly held,
and lightly exhaled breath.

Take a breath, or ten, and see.

5

Blessings of Gratitude

G ratitude is, I have discovered, a way of life, a manner of living. It is an intention and a practice, and it does take practice.

It's easier to see the holes in things, to notice them coming apart, to feel the lack, what's missing, what we cannot know or see, than to revel in what is. In the university, we are often so focused on what is in the future that we miss what is before us, what is real and now and present. Gratitude, then, is a gift of mindfulness, an intention to notice what is good without avoiding what is hurtful or missing. We can do both, holding together difficulty and awe and gratitude makes it possible to see, to hope, to work out the problems powered by grateful noticing, the energy that comes from seeing as much of the whole picture as we are able.

Gratitude is a quality of living that makes everything else better. It makes us stop striving long enough to notice where we already are, to feel awe, to grasp and relax into the concept of enough. It helps us when we are tired—scraping the bottom of the barrel—to notice what's right and good. I have even experienced that it helps us sleep better.

And gratitude is a way of living that makes us better, as a practice, as an intention, and even as a prayer. It's good, sometimes, just to make a list—out loud, or in the heart or mind— and there are several lists in these blessings, written when I, and we, most needed not to focus on the hardships but on the blessings, even one when my father was critically ill and fighting for his life, when circumstances prevented my travel to him. Gratitude helps us hold together what otherwise does not wish to be combined: grief and joy, laughter and sorrow, all and together the great realities of real life.

There are times to emphasize gratitude, even for life itself, like the breath that we count on and anticipate without having any control to ensure it. As I have written grateful prayers and blessings, I have become even more grateful, mindful and aware, in a cyclic and increasing fashion. Sometimes the details surprise us and so I often use small details—like colored paper clips, or footwear that doesn't cause blisters—to surprise students and others into (hopefully) paying attention to their own surprises, details, joys. In what prayer would you mention your shoes? I live in hope, anyway. I think that students expect prayer to be very religious, to use words that are traditional, and I have shied away—through the years of my chaplaincy career—from this kind of language, opting more often than not for a concrete kind of gratitude.

Campus communities are much more likely to be aware of—or spend time thinking about—limited budgets, buildings that need attention, failure, worry, all the things that are not going right, or that give us pause. Chaplains can help balance life by pointing to what is right, good, and thriving.

In Adversity

Gratitude in a Time of Suffering

Aware of great loss and suffering in our world,
it is good to remember to simply give thanks.

For these gifts we are grateful:
for infinite shades of springtime green,
cricket songs in grass,
healthy breakfast and shoes that fit,
rain, wind, sunshine, and moon,
dogs and skunks who never met,
good books to read,
able bodies and quick enough minds,
airplanes, emails, and dropping gasoline prices,
these fine and faithful souls,
friends aplenty,
those who lead, follow, harass, and bless.

For generous gifts and givers,
ones yet to be uncovered,
buildings with roofs and doors,
fresh paint, clean sheets,
pens that work and colored paper clips,
hospitals, nurses, pacemakers,
grace, forgiveness, breath,
family, students, teachers,
integrity and hope,
fragrant lilacs in evening,
kindness.

If the list of thanks
goes on all day,
then let it be in our hearts—
a growing sense of life,
of gratitude,
until in every moment
we can see only blessing.

Let it be, then.

We Need You

Spirit of timelessness and time,
we give thanks for those things
that are yet possible
and precious in our time—
daybreak and midnight,
a word of forgiveness,
and sometimes a song
for breath, for life.

Thanks for the sharp senses
of the timeless stirring,
for the undeniable awareness,
quick as now,
that the need of you
is the truth of us,
and your presence with us
is the truth of you
setting us free
for others,
for joy,
and for your grace.

Your Eternal Name
be praised
in the heights,
and here and now.

With open hearts, we declare it.

Mindful Thanks

We offer gratitude
for those who came before us
on whose shoulders we stand
and in whose hearts we rest.
And we dream those
who come after us.

We are mindful
of the paradox of life:
that we are sturdy souls, resilient, able, capable,
and yet also like grass, here and gone,
deep and fragile,
strong and tender,
that we matter so much
and yet all will readily adjust when we are gone,
though the love we spend and share will remain.

May we praise the maker
and offer our gifts in service of justice and peace,
and for sustaining this world, made and given,
that we love.

We raise up praise, joy, hope,
in deep gratitude for lives in this place and time.

We bow in thanks.

Blessed in the Presence of Friends

In the presence of so many friends
and such bounty,
such product and promise,
talent and passion,
we recognize our blessing.

And we remember
those we have lost but remember with full hearts,
whose stirring presence in us is a humbling blessing.

We raise our thanks,
minds, and hearts
for these blessings—
the tangible we see and hold,
the spiritual we seek with wonder,
who we are and hope one day to be,
the community of strength that enfolds us
and moves us toward new days and horizons.

Give us strength, oh Mystery,
to be a just, encouraging, and safe community,
to ever inquire and know
for wisdom's own sake,
and for the building up of the human community
we wish to serve
and to whom we belong.

Thanks be.
Praises be.
Blessed be.

In Plenty

Grateful Lives

Great mercy and love,

Thank you for daily graces—
the abundance of unearned wonders,
stirring rhythms and voices,
joy unbidden,
even the breath that rises in us now.

Thank you for meaningful work—
people worth knowing,
acts of mentoring, learning, and teaching,
friends, acceptance, value,
and even the vision of who we might yet become.

Praises for a day
to cheer the struggling,
the excelling,
the ordinary.

Be pleased now to bless us
with eyes to see the wonder
of this day
and all days,
and to live grateful lives
in thankful response.

May it be so.

Praise Unifies Us

Unifier of paradox, division, and polarity,
God of many names and none:

Bless the disparate pieces of ourselves,
our work and leisure,
our separateness and connection,
and create of us a community
where all facets of life and meaning are welcome,
honored, deeply understood,
so that every form and function of unity
might bless and delight your One Whole Spirit
and ours as well.

May it be so.

To Be Enough

Glory to you, holy wisdom,
for this day breaking over us—
light and breeze, love and breath.

Praise for the gifts we bring today—
knowledge, skill, preparation,
sharpened souls,
our passioned plans and hopes.

Tender by this moment's import,
now we offer you of your own.
At this still, holy place,
liven us with your breath
and make us a wonder to behold,
a blessing.

Like loaves and fishes,
bread and wine,
hearts, hands, lives
multiply our joy
to make it enough.

Break open hope for us
in pieces to share
around and back,
filled up,
with more to spare.

So grow our trust,
that your delight and abundance
be well and full enough.

May it be so. Amen.

Grateful Morning

For what shall we be grateful today?

For rest and waking,
songbirds, honeysuckle,
birthdays and friends who remember.

For endings that yield beginnings,
goals accomplished and better,
for generosities known and unknown,
upturned markets, needs met and exceeded,
tasks that drew and stretched and required.

For completion and celebration,
souls, hearts, and minds
that make us proud.

For wisdom, grace, and hope,
colleagues, friends of mind and heart.

For challenges yet unmet,
answers already waiting here in us,
ready.

Always richly blessed,
oh source,
turn us to bless others
and thus may we praise
you with heart and life.

May it be so.

Tangible Mercies

Tangible Mercy,
for the gift of morning
and the graces of the day,
abundance in better proportion than need,
friends and fellow travelers
who light the way,
hear our fulsome thanks.

In gratitude we ask
that you sweep us
to risks of daring beauty,
to bounties undiscovered,
to unimagined justice,
to wise offerings,
courage we could not conceive
and to joy we might not dream,
that all our asking, calling, and striving
become listening to your piercing heart
within us.

In the tenderest mercy
touch us now that
our full hearts
might become
our own hope and strength
as we follow to the brink
of reasoned love.

In us, then,
hear your own name
in every drawn and uttered
breath of praise.

This is our intention.

We Give Thanks

Thanks for the breath of morning,
this precious gift of life,
for knees even when they creak,
opposable thumbs, and coffee,
warm socks, full bellies,
three-hole punchers, blackberries, and airplanes,
books, chocolate, and wine.

Thanks for people who think we are fabulous
and friends who keep us true.

Thanks for students who love us,
those who struggle too,
and those who are yet to come,
for their supporters and families,
for our own donors and givers.

Thanks for the paths that deliver us here,
for satisfactions of work well done,
and yearnings that drive us deeper and wider.

Thanks for searching souls,
sharp minds,
open hearts,
for opportunities to use and tune them for others,
for the answers we know and seek,
leanings to follow,
and dreams to build.

Let these gifts of all we have and are
be offerings to this world,
that our glad and grateful lives
be one single trajectory
of praise.

So, it is.

Gratitude to Inspire Service
Blessing of Thanks

Baruch eta Adonai elohenu melekh ha olam
Bismillah arrahman araheem
In the name of God
whom we address and bless and acknowledge
in many languages, images, and names,
who is but One mystery and presence—

We raise grateful hearts
for the gift of life, every moment's breath,
for strength, vision, and hope.

In the midst of our abundance,
give us hearts for those who have less,
those who live with injustice, hatred, and violence.

Make us be a light for you
and our lives be our gracious service.

May our goals
always serve yours,
oh Holy mystery, and friend
for this world of need.

Let it be so then. Ameen. Ahmein.

At a Table of Bounty

Holy Mother,
we come hungry to the feast.

Hungry to honor
the selfless and active
whose caring makes them more.

Partake of this meal with us,
host and guest,
and make us tender toward those
who will still be hungry when we have feasted.

Be in our sounds of joy,
in our laughter,
in the faces around us,
in story and hearing,
and uncommon gratitude.

All the while, feed our deepest hearts and souls
with that for which we yearn—
your love and pleasure,
those who care,
work that matters,
grace that exceeds struggle,
and peace that holds it all together.
So will we be satisfied.

May it be so. Amen.

Sweet Summary of Thanks

I am grateful
for students and colleagues from whom we learn
and whom we serve,
a sense of humor,
words of respect and support,
people who tell us the truth,
leaders who know and hold us in esteem.

I am thankful
for amazing people,
family and friends who bless us,
for infinite shades of green,
magnolia blossoms in the yard,
sun and rain,
new-smelling books that offer the promise of escape or
     growth,
small movements toward justice, reconciliation, hope.

I praise
for work that measures quality,
challenges that hurt our brains,
hearts that bring us to tenderness, even tears,
lunch that offers nourishment and laughter,
the blessing of enough,
time to think,
coffee,
comfortable shoes,
friends,

breath that animates us today,
which we dare not take for granted.
Friends, I'll say it again,
friends,
those beloveds who have gone ahead of us,
time, sight, awe, excellence,
and this one moment.

May gratitude shape us
as recipients of these blessings and more,
and may their measurements be our service to others.

Let us be a sweet summary of thanks.

6

Blessings for Campus Occasions

E very institution of higher education has a distinct person-
ality, dictated by its location, purpose, leadership, history,
student body, and more. Every community has traditions
that measure and make meaning of the cycles and seasons of the
year. Some traditions and campus occasions occur annually or
every semester. Other events grow according to the need of the
moment, a new program, a new leader, ideas that blossom and take
root. The chaplain often has a part in these traditions, publicly or
privately, prayerfully or in presence. Nothing can prepare a new
chaplain for the myriad of campus occasions you might be invited
to bless or participate in, or even to help plan. I have blessed
Easter egg hunts and Halloween trick-or-treating, in addition
to new and refurbished buildings, and one 100th birthday party!
The campus occasions for which I have included blessings here
are a small representative number of the many events, meetings,
and gatherings for which I wrote and offered blessings, and these
even include my own retirement and the installation of the new
chaplain who followed me and for whom we had prayed without
knowing who it would be.

When writing these blessings, I was often inspired by the
natural world, by what I could see and feel and hear, to symbolize
what we could not yet see.

Dedications of Physical Spaces
Rededication of a Garden

As the garden outside my window underwent a renovation—was dug up, rearranged, with a bridge built over the creek and new native flowers added—I watched with daily interest as mud puddles and piles became a rock-walled and terraced garden with benches, a place of spirit, rest, and inspiration. The image from Genesis of spirit hovering over chaos into form and beauty moved me then, as it does now.

In the beginning,
out of the swirling chaos of water and darkness,
God separated the substances of earth
and created a garden
a teeming haven of life—a miracle.

Today we glory in forms
of dirt and rock, seed root, mud, and unfolded grass,
shaped from a vision to honor a history and a valley.
At the beginning, we see the form,
the shape
of what might be
in sleeping forms—
leaves fallen and turning, flowers yet to blossom,
silent roots creeping down in the dark,
working what we cannot yet know,
shades of green we have never yet seen.

May this garden grow, leap, flourish, and shine,
be fruitful and multiply,

bless and delight the eye, ear, and heart.
May it restore peace to all who enter,
call us to faith in the yet unperceived, in what might be,
until every flower, leaf, tree, and spirit
bring forth its praise in due season,
until we know for sure
that every garden, every life of soul and seed, is miracle indeed.

Now,
after the hardest work of earth and heave,
in the way of that First Gardener,
we, too, declare it good,
and together—with those before and after—praise the Maker.

Let it be so.

Dedication for a New Library

The new library—long dreamed about—was built adjacent to the chapel building, bright with floor-to-ceiling windows, areas for coffee and conversation, and housing a premier children's literature collection with tiny chairs and tables, rockers and tea sets. It remains a gathering place for students and the university community. The symbolism of shared visions of spiritual and intellectual insight is fixed in brick, glass, page, and the ever-newest technology. The dedication was immediately preceded by a pelting rain and a rainbow.

Oh Breath Eternal,
your word over chaos
shaped water, light, creature, flesh,
burst into blossom profusion,
diaphanous rainbow, and song.
Be praised in thought, word, and deed,
in dream, sweat, and grit.

Bless now, we pray, this house of learning, books, and words
and those who labor in it,
to teach, learn, and love the true.
May we find here unity over babel,
humility over precedence,
and serve your will's progress
and never stumble.
May your spirit hover over and within this library
as over all our houses,
creating residences of life and laughter.

May all who here seek wisdom

be summoned by her favored face
to serve justice, speak truth, love adventure,
until all our words,
printed, matrixed, digitized, danced, and dreamed,
become one resounding holy word—
first and last—
Alleluia.

May it be so. Amen.

A Multifaith Center Dedication

On a warm May afternoon, when the multifaith center pavilion was a series of connected steel girders rising from a mud pit, I went up into the oculus of the building, the highest point, in a cherry picker, wearing a neon lime-green vest and a yellow hard hat. I attached a laminated sheet of images of the world's religions on the steel structure, that now abides under the sheetrock and paint, dedicating the building, and this "eye" of light and hope for the prayers of all peoples, cultures, and traditions.

> Blessed are you, Holy One, ruler of the universe and the
>   university.
> All your wonders praise you,
> and your seeking servants bless you.
>
> In wisdom, you made all things to give you glory:
> the rain and moon and sun,
> the shadow of Venus,
> the scent of magnolia blossom,
> the red dirt as it dries,
> steel beams rising.
>
> Bestow your presence again
> that we may witness your love and blessing
> in this structure
> for your glory.
>
> May our use of this space,
> and its presence here in our grounds
> increase our search for meaning,

impact our finding hope, strength, and love,
inspire shared vision, understanding, respect,
and deepen the insights of diverse and inclusive lives.

Build the soul of this house
with open windows, the wealth of opportunity,
with light, fellowship, love,
peace, and joy,
that we may know you here.

Praise be for the rising of
this temple-school-home
and for every simultaneous lifting of our hearts.

May it be so. Amen.

Blessings for Groups and Individuals
Blessing Silent Teachers

Silent teachers are those who have given their bodies for medical student dissection and education, an honorable, intentional, and holy gift for those who learn from them what no book can teach, and whose healing knowledge is used with thousands of patients in their practices.

Creator,
we make praise for the gift of life itself,
for the shapes that make us unique and whole,
for the energy and breathing love that daily sustains.

We honor the silent teachers
whose holy lives now instruct
these caregivers.
Blessed gift: a human body, a donor,
a teacher and blessing.
Be present here too—
breath of life and thanks—
that we may be tender and caring,
capable and clear,
that awe would always be near
in the presence of each sacred being here, living and dead.

Bless now those who grieve,
that their tears would be holy too,
and that their comfort—and ours—would be love
that ever holds a human form.

Let it be gratitude that makes holy the gift,
giver, recipient, learning, and knowledge
and may we all together
serve your healing purposes for the world.

This is our grateful hearts' desire.

A Blessing for Medical Students

Thanks be to the God of many names—
for the gift of this day of beauty, for life rising in us,
and the stirring magnificence and mystery of the human
    body.

We offer praise for those
who have given the best of themselves,
to engage and learn,
to come rejoicing to this day.

Strengthen them to always learn and grow,
to seek excellence and kindness,
to listen and hear,
to push the boundaries of fairness for the sake of justice
for those they serve,
to become leaders in their field
as we already know them to be.
May the lives they touch prove them to be the healers
they have desired and trained to become.

Give them the blessings of supportive colleagues,
work to intrigue and challenge them,
joy to guard them,
and spirit to ground their self and service.
May your presence flow through them
to be agents of wholeness and hope
that this world so desperately needs.

May you ever be praised through them,
and through us.

Let it be so, then.

Blessing Before a Justice Speaker

Bismallah Al Rahman, Al Rahim.
In the name of Compassion and Mercy—
breathless from the pace of April,
yearning for culminations and celebrations of May,
with miles and pages, ideas
and dramas, churning before us—

We take a breath
and recollect ourselves
as those honored to teach and learn,
as seekers of wisdom, insight, liberation,
joyous at having a part in rich lives well spent,
the shaping of tough compassionate souls to act for the poor,
work for justice,
heal the creation,
turn to tenderness,
and to rejoice in the wholeness of it all.

As we return,
resuming wits, hearts, and direction
to the well-ordered fray—

summon us to be the blessing
we now seek:
to share,
to welcome,
to serve and change our world
with creative action and courageous wonder
for all that could finally be.

Make it so, then, for us here,
and for all of us.

Yes, please.

Blessing for a 100th Birthday for an Esteemed and Retired Staff Member

Eternal God of Ageless years,
creator and author of every day,
of life and breath itself—
accept our praise now
for the long and splendid life of
your wonderful creation K.,
for the lives she has touched
over all these years.

Remind us today
that your wonders never cease
as we celebrate the wonder
of 100 years.

We give you honor
for her wisdom and intelligence,
for the range of her service, her humor, her stories, her
  family,
for the gifts of her sharing
over years, generations, history.

Now grant her
the gift of peace of mind and heart
that she may live all her moments fully in honor
and that her life would continue to bless each and all of us,
and you.

We make our prayer
and give our praise
to the glory of your wonderful and Holy Name.

Amen.

A Gathering of Alumni

Holy Ethereal,
very present
source of our truest dreams:

Be praised
in beauty,
sun-warmed meadows,
shaded valleys,
the meaning and challenge of these days.

Be honored
by those who inspire us,
friends who know and love us,
challengers who force us beyond ourselves,
and those who advocate for
justice, artistry, and integrity.

Sustain us in strength
for challenge and opportunity,
for laughter and longing,
in ability and effort,
through affection and respect,
always tuned to your own befriending.

May it be so
in all our days.

Anniversary of a Secret Service Society

We have been carriers of light,
walkers, hidden, bearing the treasure of
aspiration, hope, truth—
yearning thus to always see a flame's reflection.

We are not the light keepers
but entreat that great light
to fill us,
move and shine in us,
to be the reflection in our own eyes
and further press us toward what might be.

Do bless us now with the fires of your cleansing,
revealing healing love in these faces,
hope for centuries more.
Inspire us to live as we know best,
to work for justice here and there,
and to live to bless with light and hope.
This home we love,
these friends whose hearts rise with ours,
and the walks from here we inhabit.

Let it be so. Amen.

A Rainy Commencement Weekend

In the case of outside commencements, some ask the chaplain to pray it doesn't rain. There are lots of things we want to rain down, instead of water, and many appreciate a sense of humor about the weather and other blessings that might come pouring down.

Holy One,
King of the Universe
and of our tiny corner of the earth,
we respectfully ask
if you would bless us with no rain.

Of course,
at every moment,
in rain or shine,
gray or sunny,
we give thanks to you alone.

So if it rains,
let it be gracious plenty:
students, donors,
rising markets,
stable endowments,
and the tricks of balance.

Or if it pours,
let it be blessing,
wonder, gratitude, awe,
marvel, and grace.

If we hear thunder
or see the flash of light in the sky,
let it be the brilliance of justice,
the best of all the rights we share,
sparks of genius for this and every moment
of struggle and bravery.

If it's any of these,
then let it roll right down
and pour, pelt,
come like cats, dogs, sheets, buckets
so that we need not umbrellas
but open hands and hearts to grasp your blessing.

And in the end,
may our grateful praise
and gathered blazing hearts
be all the shining warmth
we need for tomorrow
and for today.

Let it be. Amen.

Blessing Graduates

Spirit of stability and home,
we give thanks for our lives,
for this gray day,
gifts of love from your hand,
for this place we honor and hold in our hearts,
and for these graduates we present to the world.

We bless their accomplishments,
their growth in soul, body, and mind,
the support of their families and friends,
the roots they have put here,
and the awesome and varied journeys they now undertake.

Spirit of the pilgrim road,
assure us of your slow and holy work in our lives,
that we may trust you all our days,
even in storms,
seek you in every way station
and in all the surprising places we find ourselves.

Spirit of every uncertainty and suspense,
assure us that nothing is wasted in your way,
that every success and failure leads us
to where and who we are supposed to be,
and that every moment you are present with us in love.

Mark these pilgrims with the blessings of your joy,
that their gratitude makes them hospitable and just,

to love and protect the earth,
to serve those in need,
to seek good and resist evil,
and to remake the structures of injustice
into the vision of equity and love that you dream for us.

May our lives and hearts
always bring your delight,
now and in the days before us.

Blessed be!

Retirement Blessing

Sustaining God,
this evening we gather to give thanks for P.,
for her work and service among us,
for her spirit,
and to pray rich blessing on her days of retirement.

Thanks be for P.,
for her gentle persuasive spirit,
for her love of the Oxford comma, and her meticulous and
keen eye for copy editing,
for her steadfast work all these long, happy, and strenuous years,
for the many relationships cultivated and enjoyed on our
behalf,
for the friends she has made for and with us,
and the quiet strong presence of grace she has been in our
midst,
and for all the ways she has made us better people.

We ask blessing on the days to come
that they would be full of rest and
all the pursuits that bring joy.
May good health be her foundation
and her family and friends her occupation.
May she know of our love, even from the distance she hopes
to keep.

We raise thanks for this meal that we now share,
for the chance to gratefully acknowledge the difference
one life makes among us.

Bless us with your generous presence,
and let our celebration be music to your ears.

The God of Love be praised.

Amen.

Fun Days

Family Weekend Football

Today we celebrate and bless
family of every kind,
clan, tribe, and team,
whose names we share
whose concerns we bear
and who show us who we are.

We raise grateful hearts for those whose
love understands and transcends our flaws,
those who believe in us better than we can ourselves,
whose insight challenges us to be better,
those whose sacrifices give us opportunity
and whose nets of support keep us from falling.

We ask for safety in game and travel,
for joy in reunion,
and conversations that lift us up.
We ask that honor be our guide
and that the journey would be sweet.

Now, we ask you kindly, please give us a victory
and a high road,
as we give our highest effort, our joyous cheering,
and this most happy day.

Let this be.

Halloween Thanks

We saved the best for last,
all dressed up in bandanas and tiaras.
Like children
with sweaty hands,
we clutch the bowing handle
of a filling pail.

Yours is a hilltop home,
bright in the dark way,
making us blink and giggle
in happy hope.

Your door stands already open,
our parcels suddenly brimming full
with rich delights,
sweets, treasures, happy laughing.
And in the tasting of our bounty,
all the generous hearts and hands have been yours.
We find that you have
blessed, protected, shared, and increased the gifts.
You tricked us
and roamed with us
all the way and more.

So thanks, and double thanks.

Student Award Banquet

Was it sufficient
that, as we gathered,
we drew deep breaths
and relished the scents of spring—
of leaf and flower—
and raised our faces to the sun
and breeze
and noted, but for a moment,
the gifts of the universe?

Would it be enough
if we looked around us
and noticed our friends,
the pride, the offering, the hope
of those who know us well
and who love, support, believe,
and whose lives matter in every way
to us and to our precious world?

Is it enough
that ice rings in glasses,
laughter rises to the rafters,
the pride and hope of the year
offers itself
in these friends,
this joy,
that an eternal Friend
hosts the meal,

the community,
the blessing,
and the way forward from here?

May it be so.

Blessings for Leadership

A Blessing of Leadership

Heavenly Father and Mother,
you are our help in ages past,
Savior, spirit, maker,
fearful, wonderful, ageless,
tender, and sweet.
You we honor and bless
as grand beyond our senses—
far and high and wise.

We know you too as friend,
in the rough and tumble of thunder,
the play of electric light and breeze and leaf,
gifts to sustain and more,
students of grace and diligence,
respect beyond our abilities,
listening leaders,
strength to serve and learn
and teach and grow.

You befriend in graces,
blessings of which we are only vaguely aware,
hopes we have not yet dreamed,
in time and place,
in work and play and challenge.

You are friend too
in faces and prayer,

circles of light and laughter,
celebrations of yesterday's hopes and tomorrow's dreams,
lifted eyes and hearts,
and in the precious abundance
of unfathomable love.

Befriend us always. Amen.

A Founder's Day Blessing

We bow deeply to Eternal Thou.
In silence we remember those who are present
only in ineffable light.

Eternal Present,
we—your gathered friends, quarrelers, refugees, and lovers—
seek the remembrance that we too
reside in, from, and toward eternity
with all who seek, embrace, and follow what is true.
Do thou re-create in us—
who divide so easily before, during, and after—
this wisdom that burns from age to age
and dream to waking.

This once yearly and more
let us recall with honor and respect
who led the way
for us and those who follow us,
to give thanks for timeless inspiration,
to fit it again to ourselves,
to see anew wisdom's vision.

Be praised
in light,
in our lives,
and in our one whole life.

May it be so.

A Vision Gathering

Holy Friend,
you love us as we are.
May your divine delight draw us ever nearer
to who we might be for you.

Accept our grateful thanks as we raise hearts, minds, and eyes
to the vision that calls us still into being,
a spirited community of learning we are
and would be.
Grace us to give ourselves over again to that dream
of being a just, safe, joyous, and challenging community
to make friends
with disciplines and ideas,
with classes, faculty, laborers, and labor,
with these hills, valleys, pastures, and streams that feed our
    hearts,
with this precious and dangerous world of ours,
and with the souls who inhabit it with us.

Stir in us such a deepening
of care that the heart of our friendship
might be present,
visible, tangible, profound and lovely.
May the love we find in education
become beauty
and freedom
and service.

May it be blessing not for our own only,
but for the widest earth
and for your great joy.

May it be so. Amen.

Summer Trustees Blessing

Oh Holy Beloved,
we yearn for you,
first and most deeply.

This, too, is what we desire and ask—
more and finer students,
balanced budgets,
refurbished buildings and vital programs,
happy faculty and first-rate scholarship,
raises all around,
fat endowments and thin conflicts,
smooth sidewalks and greenest grass,
stable and loving families and communities,
effortless and generous alumni giving,
successful strategies,
abundant scholarships,
softer, slower days of summer,
sneezeless pollen and uninterrupted sleep.

We know we need you,
your blessing, unity, and delight,
more than we can know, desire, or ask.

And so, we invite you, here and now,
to lend your clarity, perspective,
your justice, hope, and wisdom to these deliberations,
decisions, and people.

And even when it's not the whole truth—
that we yearn for you above all else—
make it so in and for us
in the sure belief that you are yearning for us,
teaching us to desire what draws us to you,
first and deepest,
already with and in us,
already at work, already making us yours.

May it be so. Amen.

After a Capital Campaign

Eternal Friend,
we gather here
twice blessed.

Blessed are we in receiving the rich bounty of life
and its enjoyments:
eyes and legs, mind and heart and life,
the belonging and love of this place and family
that enriches our soul
with friends, laughter, and challenge.

Blessed again are we
in giving back
to efforts which inspire—
not the duty,
but the glad privilege
of upholding and sustaining
the first and lasting gift.

So twice blessed by you,
we toast our doubled joy,
to feast and laugh,
to rejoice in buildings and projects
funded and finished,
to dream of other gifts as fine,
to celebrate and commit ourselves to still greater graces.

Be here, in presence, host and guest,
and hear us as we
give thanks
and thanks again.

Amen.

Blessing for a New President

Giver of all our years,
holiness of all times:
for this beginning—and all new beginnings—
our hearts rise in gratitude.

We ask your blessing on our new president.

Inspire in her person your likeness:
innocent strength, exuberant joy,
deep attentive listening,
wisdom, understanding, and clarity,
persistent caring, tough beauty,
a nurtured family life, and even a sunny disposition.

May she be known for
her agile and deep heart and mind,
the true vision commanding and calling her,
lives she touches across many years of fruitful service,
the happy laughter her leadership inspires.

Protect her from illness, accident, fatigue,
from criticism aimed to injure,
from despair, heartache, and overwork that taxes joy.

Move in the hearts of all
who offer themselves as part of this community—
inspire kindness and justice we cannot yet conceive,
courage that appears impossible,
commitments we have not yet imagined.

Eternal thou, be lifted up in the eyes and life and work
of N.,
and may this day stand as the threshold of your yet
richest blessing.
Send us forward in deep hope
to meet our future
and to become our best selves.

Visit us with the presence of grace
on this momentous day
and on every day,
that all we are and do and make and hope
may be but one resounding word of praise
for the One we aim to bless.

Alleluia.

A Chaplain's Departure

This is a prayer I offered to the faculty at the final meeting before my retirement.

Finding words for the end
is harder even than our first awkward meeting.
I will carry you in my heart,
with the deep blessings of this place,
in all we have learned and grown,
In equivalent ways, I leave part of myself with you.

I have loved you.

At the end, I am grateful.
Here is a rendering of thanks I offer
to you, and to the life-giving breath among us.

I am grateful for you,
for the fierce fire in your souls for justice and equity,
for the love of learning that founds us,
for caring spirits,
for the beauty enfolding us,
for history, tradition, correction, and thoughtful innovation,
for planning and serendipity,
strategic joy and nourishing reflection,
for every urge to do better,
for those who inspire us to love,
and serve,
and from whom we ask the world.

I am thankful that we pray, dance, eat, and walk together,
that every generous part matters to the whole we seek,
that we know we make a lasting impact.

May gratitude
bind us together and make all our years meaningful.
May our sacred mission keep us directed and whole,
empower our love,
strengthen us in grueling days,
and bring joy at the finish line
of the year and of this particular career.
And may all of us be a rich blessing for this desperate world.

Blessing for a New Chaplain's Installation

Grateful we are,
enormously,
for the gift of life and its abundance,
for community, pastoral gifts, searches,
for all the yeses that bring us to this moment.
Accept our thanks for K.,
for her strong and capable arrival.

Bless her
as she accepts the responsibility of her office and leadership.
Give her courage to do the hard thing,
to find joy,
to tell the truth,
and challenge what needs changing,
to perceive the needs and capacity of those around her,
and to lead into the unknown future.

We ask for her
patience and persistence,
new understandings and commitments to justice and inclusion,
creative new avenues and access to spiritual life,
as she loves real human beings.
Give her power as she names the pain
and points us to hope—
always the chaplain's work.

In it all, may your grace cover her
and nourish her soul and spirit.

Hold her center open for the living of grace and truth.
May the love that flows though her be divine in origin and
 intent,
making her fair, just, and whole
as a chaplain, human being, leader, and member of this
 community.
Guard her joy and protect her family.

We give thanks, in advance, for her success,
for the joy of her presence,
in all the years ahead through abundance and challenge.

Through it all,
in good and difficult times,
assure her, deep down, that she is enough,
that your spirit multiplies
and makes sacred each gift
sufficient to the moment and need.

And we pray for our community,
that we become ready for her truth,
that there be yeses here among us,
courage to embrace change and challenge,
and a continuous sense of care for each other.

May the Holy One be present in this blessing,
over this year of change, assessment, new beginnings,
over all we leave behind
and the new we receive,
and over the unfolding years
as they bless and grow us.

May the blessing of love hold us together,
give us strength,
and offer us peace,
that all our lives and works may praise and delight
you, oh Holy One.
May it be so, today and in all the days to come.

Acknowledgments

Chaplaincy is lonely work. In the early days there were usually just one of us on any given campus. In my more than 40 years of chaplaincy, the chaplaincy associations—first, the National Association of College and University Chaplains (NACUC) and now the Association of Chaplaincy and Spiritual Life in Higher Education (ACSLHE, pronounced "axle") have offered invaluable support and learning, collegial friendships, and inspiration. A truer or more urgently needed support system never existed, and I am grateful to have had a hand in leadership of these two wonderful organizations of fine human beings who have become friends.

I am ever grateful for the love and encouragement of my parents, Wayne and Frances Fuller, for their willingness to live and raise their children in another country, language, religion, and culture. My love for other cultures and spiritual paths is surely a reflection of their commitment to love and learn across boundaries. They believed in me, in my calling to ministry, my abilities, and my need to honor religions besides my own. My mother was my first writing teacher and taught me to love the creative impact of words.

I thank, from the bottom of my heart, the universities that allowed me to bless them—students, faculty, and staff—over the years.

And without the encouragement, support, urging, and even prodding of my beloved Jan Therien, these blessings would still be sitting in file folders in boxes in the basement or somewhere encoded deep in a computer chip.